PURGING
Racism
from
CHRISTIANITY

PURGING Racism from CHRISTIANITY

Freedom & Purpose Through Identity

Jefferson D. Edwards, Jr.

ZondervanPublishingHouse

Grand Rapids, Michigan

A Division of HarperCollinsPublishers

Purging Racism from Christianity
Copyright © 1996 by Jefferson D. Edwards

Requests for information should be addressed to:

ZondervanPublishingHouse
Grand Rapids, Michigan 49530

Library of Congress Cataloging-in-Publication Data

Edwards, Jefferson D., 1951–
    Purging racism from Christianity / Jefferson D. Edwards, Jr.
      p.   cm.
    ISBN: 0-310-20195-0 (pbk.)
      1. Racism—Religious aspects—Christianity—Controversial literature.
    2. Afro-Americans—Religion.   3. Blacks—Religion.   4. Evangelicalism.
    I. Title.
    BT734.2.E38   1996
    261.8'348—dc20   96-17623
                                                    CIP

Printed in the United States of America

---

96 97 98 99 00 01 02 03 /❖ DH/ 10 9 8 7 6 5 4 3 2 1

I dedicate this book to the many people who have gone before me in the liberation of people throughout the earth, and to those who are now answering the call of liberation, especially in modern-day Christianity.

This book is especially dedicated to the church in South Africa, the West Indies, and in the United States. I have personally been involved with the church community in these nations and islands for more than twenty years. I have seen and experienced the long-term effects of racism on the church. I have heard the cry—I have seen the affliction. I am acquainted with the sorrows of oppression in these places.

Now I pray by the grace of God and the power of the Holy Spirit that I can be used, perhaps through this book, to help deliver you.

Contents

Part 4: The Direction

Part 5: The Problems, the Rewards

Acknowledgments

Special acknowledgments go to Bheki Gamedze from Swaziland, Africa, and Neville Owens from Jamaica, West Indies. Along with my own personal observations, they have greatly added to my understanding of colonialism abroad and its effects on people. As ministers of the Gospel, they have been able to experience firsthand the long-term effects of colonialism's oppression and the spirit behind it, while remaining free from its indoctrination through the power of the kingdom of God, which they represent. I count them as important colaborers in kingdom business.

I would also like to acknowledge Bishop Johnnie Smith of Greenville, South Carolina, who asked questions in his television interview that I had never been asked before. His questions helped me to sort out and organize thoughts and understandings that were within me but that I had never before expressed until his wisdom pulled them out. Thank you, Bishop, for asking me the right things at the right time. Thank you also for mentioning my name in the right place, at the right time, which resulted in the writing of this book.

Special recognition also goes to Dorothy Chaplain, an elder in my church. She is a multi-talented woman, with many responsibilities, who added to them by taking on the tedious task of transcribing my tapes. Four of the chapters are based on her transcriptions of messages I have preached. Thank you, Dorothy, for doing what had to be done with such joy and clarity of purpose.

As always, I especially want to thank my wife, Debra, and my two daughters, Honesty Joy and Emiah Meshel, along with my claimed daughter, Sandra Truelove. They are my immediate family and play such an important part in anything that I do, including the writing of this book.

Introduction

I started writing this book in Johannesburg, South Africa, 10,000 miles from home, because of what I saw there and what I had lived. It was there, in a country where organized racism and the spirit of oppression for blacks had remained untouched for more than three hundred years, that I began to sense the direction for this book. I began to see so clearly how important the "identity" of a people is to how they survive in this world, how they overcome oppression.

South Africa is a nation just emerging from the bonds of legal racism. Almost all blacks in Johannesburg, regardless of their status in life, are corralled into one section of the city to keep them separated from whites. That section is Soweto. It's where I was ministering. Walk down a street with me and you'll see signs of crime and fear of crime— homes with high walls around the yards, fences with barbed wire, iron bars on windows and doors for security. We pass the home of an upper-middle-class South African family next door to a four-room flat, then come to a two-room hut next to a middle-class home. The signs of poverty, of mere subsistence living, are everywhere.

Now stroll through a white neighborhood in Johannesburg, a utopia by comparison, with guards to keep the peace and enforce the laws. Blacks—any blacks—are allowed only if they have a worker's pass and only between certain hours.

Now come with me to church on Sunday. Especially hurtful to me was how the religious community in South Africa not only failed to stop the country's system of racism, which they call apartheid, but accepted and encouraged it. Here, too, the barriers are very real.

But the situation was about to change. In that first month of my writing, Nelson Mandela was elected president of the Republic of South Africa. He had been imprisoned for twenty-seven years for his resistance to the all-white government. Originally charged with "treason" but acquitted, Nelson Mandela spent those years convicted of "sabotage," sentenced to life in prison.

Just imagine. From prison to the presidency. *This is an answer to many prayers, the result of the blood, sweat, and tears of many black and white South Africans*, I thought, when the election victory was announced. But I knew that political victory was only a first step, a very small step. The real work of dismantling the attitudes of racism and oppression that blanketed the country lay ahead. For you cannot legislate true freedom.

To gain equality, the blacks in South Africa must learn their true "identity" from the Word of God. The church of Jesus Christ should have led the way in the process of spiritual and racial healing in South Africa. But it did not. White churches even participated in the oppressive system of apartheid and in fact, greatly benefited from it.

Five months after President Mandela's election, a black church leader there told me that the dismantling of apartheid, in general, was a cooperative effort throughout the country—except in the religious system. Strong resistance was coming from whites in the community of faith. One denomination that has separate black and white congregations tried to become the leader in breaking down the walls of racism and oppression. The effort fell apart when some of the white ministers decided not to participate because the black churches outnumbered the white. Not wanting to be a minority, these white ministers left to form a separate denomination, thereby continuing apartheid and discrimination in the religious world.

One well-known church, which is comprised of both black and white South Africans, professes to be interracial, but blacks congregate in one service on Sunday mornings, whites in another. They meet together, in the same worship service, *only* when something big happens in the denomination or a well-known minister or singer from the United States arrives to minister. What hypocrisy! Obviously racism is alive and well in the South African community of faith.

And in the community of faith in the United States. Come with me six months later to Greenville, Mississippi, to a state still recognized for its racist practices, where I finished writing this book. While I minister at Pilgrim Rest Baptist Church, Martin Luther King III is leading a "Poor People's" fact-finding tour in the Mississippi Delta. His father, Dr. Martin Luther King Jr., visited this same Mississippi Delta during another "Poor People's" march more than twenty-five years before. What did they both find? Poor people. Lots of black poor people. Nothing has changed. The poverty is still here. The attitudes of racism are still present. Mr. Jim Crow still walks the Mississippi

Delta. Oh, he might walk with a cane now, but he's still hanging out. In fact, slavery was still legal in Mississippi until 1995. That's when legislation abolishing slavery was finally adopted.

Let's face it. Too many blacks and whites look at each other through "race-colored" glasses.

But that, too, is about to change, for God is speaking to us in the black community. God has a message for us that can bring long-term change.

Racism and oppression are from the very pit of hell. Now is the time for us to stand up and speak out, to put a stop to the undercurrent of racism that we so politely tolerate. Only the church can strike the lethal blow at the very roots of racism and oppression, hatred and bigotry. Only the church, through its teaching and yielding to the work of the Holy Spirit, can change the minds and attitudes of people.

The church is built upon the truth that Jesus is the Christ, the Son of the Living God. The gates of hell will not prevail against it. The church, through the power and the presence of the Holy Spirit, is our only hope for extinguishing the flames of racism.

We have been on this path of destruction for too long. It's time to purge racism from Christianity.

Part 1

Why Identity Is Important

Chapter 1

Identity: A Basic Process in Confronting Racism

Identity, or in my case, the restoring of identity, is one of the first processes the Lord uses to liberate a people from oppression, so they can be free to respond to him without reservation. One of our main problems as black people is that we don't really know who we are as a people. We have been raped of a clear sense of our identity by others, those who have kept us in an inferior or subservient role throughout the world.

We have lost our sense of purpose and destiny as it relates to God. Our neighborhoods are infested with gang warfare, high crime, drive-by shootings, and a high incidence of drug abuse, murder, family breakdown, and displacement of our men in prison.

We have been told all our lives that we are inferior, subservient to whites, that we are dumb, cannot learn, even that we are without a soul, the latter by a religious world wanting to theologically justify slavery and the oppression of black people. We sit in classrooms thinking we are inferior to whites whenever a lesson is hard to understand or we struggle with a new concept, never realizing that white students are struggling too. We have been led to believe that even if we were to succeed on our own merit in the white world, we would still not be qualified. We would be looked at as the "token" black. White people still would not be willing to accept us as bosses, as supervisors, as teachers. Or, in most cases, the better-paying jobs would simply not be "available." Just as an apartment or a house is "not available," even today, with all the legislation in place to ban the practice. Instead, we are grouped in inner-city ghettoes, far from the pristine white suburban communities. In fact, police can be called when a black man is in a white neighborhood after a certain hour. In some neighborhoods, at any hour.

Defeated by this inferiority mind-set, too many of us shuffle our feet, walk away with our heads down, limping away as wounded soldiers. We walk away because we don't know who we are or where we're going.

At the other extreme of black society is the growing minority who have developed a hatred and frustration because of the effects of racism. This attitude of defiance is seen in more and more blacks who are trying to prove to whites that we are as good, as intelligent, and as capable as they are. But these blacks never pursue purpose—they are too busy pursuing approval from or revenge against those who have labeled us "inferior."

A LOST HERITAGE

There is a tremendous need to restore to black people a sense of identity that carries with it a sense of self-worth and self-esteem, a sense of purpose—a reason for living. Normally, a person has a knowledge of heritage from stories told in the family, the passing down of information from one generation to the next. I should have had a sense of being a part of a proud heritage that stretches back in time and holds promise for future generations. I should have grown up knowing that my family was good at something. And I should have learned how to do whatever that "something" was. With this built-in knowledge I would have been helped in shaping my future, my desires, and my motivations in life. But I did not know. My heritage was interrupted by the immorality of slavery.

If I had followed the course set for me by a society that benefits from depriving me of my heritage and, ultimately, of my destiny, I would have missed my purpose in life. Instead of preaching for an end to racism, I could have been left to hang out, bent on a course of self-destruction. I could have been one of the thousands of black men caged in prison.

I was lucky. I was blessed. I found out who I am—my identity—and gained my sense of purpose and destiny as it relates to God. My mission is to point the way for others to do the same.

From a historical perspective, from God's perspective, we as black people in the United States must first understand that we have lost our sense of purpose and destiny. Together we can change that. We must change that. Without the intervention of the Lord through his Spirit in my life, I would have missed my identity. I would have missed my purpose in life.

My brothers and sisters, isn't it about time that you are freed from your inferiority complex? Knowing who you are is the beginning of the liberation of your mind. Knowing who you are is the first process by which the shackles of oppression are broken and a sense of purpose and destiny is restored. I know that you may be beaten, broken, battered, tattered, even incarcerated by an oppressive society, but you are not alone in dealing with the issue of identity.

Jesus Christ can identify with your struggles because he, too, lived in an oppressive society—the Roman Empire. He, too, had a problem with identity, though his was different than ours. His problem wasn't that he didn't know who he was. No, Jesus knew exactly who he was and from whom he had come, and that's what got him into trouble.

Chapter 2

The Rise of Racism in American Christianity

Long before cannons fired over Fort Sumter, civil war raged within the American church. The issue was slavery, the immoral trafficking in humans.

Going back as far as 1775, slavery had begun to divide the American colonies. A group in Pennsylvania that year founded the first American abolition organization to free the more than 450,000 slaves in the colonies. But they had little effect. Slavery continued. By the time of the Civil War, there were more than four million blacks held as slaves. But the belief that slavery was wrong—immoral— was spreading.

Where was the church during all this debate? Right in the middle of it. By 1830, slavery had become so sharp and powerful an issue in the United States that Christian groups and denominations were torn apart. Why?

Church members in the North had begun a war against slavery on moral grounds.

The "Underground Railroad" was helping runaway slaves to reach freedom in the North and in Canada.

During the 1830s, the famous revivalist Charles Finney converted thousands to Christianity, and many joined the crusade against slavery.

Cotton production, which depended on slave labor in the South, became increasingly profitable and essential to the South's economy, causing plantation owners to resist all efforts to free their slaves.

In 1831, Virginia slave and preacher Nat Turner led a violent revolt that killed fifty-seven whites. Southerners, already against losing their laborers for economic reasons, now became fearful of the attempts to free the thousands of slaves surrounding them. Black slaves accounted for almost a third of the country's population at the time. But because most of the slaves were in the South, blacks outnumbered whites in some states.

Also in 1831, fiery abolitionist William Lloyd Garrison of Boston began publishing his anti-slavery newspaper, *The Liberator.* Unfortunately, his heated attacks on slavery only hardened Southern attitudes.

In reaction, the Virginia legislature in 1831 made it illegal to teach slaves to read and write. Virginia wasn't the only state. All but four slave states had similar laws.

Slaves were even prohibited from testifying in court against whites.

In 1832, the New England Anti-Slavery Society was formed by Boston abolitionists.

The World's Anti-Slavery Convention opened in London in 1840.

The immorality of slavery had become an explosive issue. Three major Protestant denominations—Presbyterian, Methodist, and Baptist—were torn apart over slavery or issues related to slavery. These denominational divisions also fractured political parties, fraternal orders, families, corporations, partnerships, and American society in general, ultimately dividing the nation. By 1837, the anti-slavery societies that had existed across the South had disappeared. Southern abolitionists fled to the North for safety.

The church division helped to reshape the American church. Christianity in the South and its counterpart in the North headed in opposite directions. Important new denominations, such as the Southern Baptist Convention, which formed in the South, actually supported and endorsed the institution of slavery. Southern believers required a close, literal reading of Scripture, then used those literal meanings to promote erroneous interpretations that defended slavery. Northerners, who emphasized the underlying principles of the Scriptures, such as God's love for humanity, increasingly promoted social causes and an anti-slavery attitude.

The religious world in the South, by justifying the enslavement of black people in the United States, actually set the scene for the secular world to pass laws that protected slave owners' rights. Many Southerners believed that "abolition and Union could not coexist and, given the two races, slavery was a 'positive good.'" Southern church leaders and theologians began to develop a strong and systematic—though erroneous—scriptural defense of slavery. The belief among Southern Christians was that slavery, in one

Baptist minister's words, "stands as an institution of God." Southerners attacked Northern abolitionists for their "rationalism," "infidelity," and "meddling spirit."

The Presbyterian Church is one example of how Christian thinking, instead of standing up for what was right, changed through the years to go along with the attitudes of the day. As early as 1818, the Presbyterians, in a religious act of diplomacy at their General Assembly, unanimously declared that "the voluntary enslaving of one part of the human race by another" is "utterly inconsistent with the law of God." Ironically, the same assembly members upheld a decision to depose a Presbyterian minister because he held anti-slavery views. Twenty-seven years later, in 1845, the Presbyterian General Assembly approved a new position paper calling slavery "a biblical institution." What happened to slavery being "utterly inconsistent with the law of God"?

Many so-called "great" preachers in church history were strong advocates of slavery. This was especially true in the South, because slavery was a strong part of the economy of the South. The love of money was at the root of all kinds of evil.

Nor did black slaves receive true Christianity. When allowed to attend a church service, slaves were taught a religion that aided the power structure of the day but was not an accurate presentation of the Word of God and the kingdom of God. These so-called "men of God" preached a gospel that embraced the practices of unjust discrimination (slavery), racism, hatred, and oppression. Slaves were taught that it was their "duty" to obey their masters, that they would receive their reward in the hereafter.

Most religious bureaucrats of the day tried to keep slavery out of public discussions and bring peace through silence. But there was to be no peace. Within a few years, the three major denominations split.

When the American church became divided on the issue of slavery, a strong cord tying the North and South together was cut. Ninety-four percent of all Southern churches belonged to one of the three denominations that split. Before 1844, the Methodist Church was even the largest organization in the country (excluding the federal government). With the split over slavery, the South suddenly, in a religious sense, was set adrift from the Union. And its churches, instead of standing up for righteousness regarding the issue of slavery, sunk into a fearful and silent stupor.

One Kentucky senator, Henry Clay, declared that the religious denominational division because of the issue of slavery was the greatest source of danger to America. He was right. The Civil War was only sixteen years away. And the underlying cause was slavery.

FREEDOM

On January 1, 1863, in the middle of the Civil War, President Abraham Lincoln signed the Emancipation Proclamation, freeing all slaves in areas that had seceded from the Union.

But attitudes of racism that could have been stopped at that point continued, because laws can't change attitudes and beliefs. Only God can.

A century later, in 1965, many blacks were rioting in the streets of America's big cities to get the rights that had been promised by Lincoln's "sacred" document, basic rights that are taken for granted by so many in this country. Legal slavery in the United States had long since been abolished, but true equality and freedom hadn't even begun. Although freedom is an inherent right of all human beings, I am convinced that freedom cannot be legislated, except by God. Where was the church in those hundred years after 1863? Where is the church today?

Some respected historians and theologians have written that honorable, ethical, and God-fearing people were on both sides of our country's debate on the issue of slavery. But can one be ethical, moral, Bible-believing, and God-fearing *and* embrace sin at the same time?

> With it [the tongue] we bless our God and Father, and with it we curse men, who have been made in the similitude of God. Out of the same mouth proceed blessing and cursing. My brethren, these things ought not to be so. Does a spring send forth fresh water and bitter from the same opening? (James 3:9–11 NKJV)

More white Christians should have been prepared to confront the sin of racism and oppression in the 1860s before the Civil War and again, in the 1960s, during the civil rights movement. Those few who did speak out against racism in the 1960s were stepping out of the ranks of the white majority. Some "freedom riders" were beaten, even killed, in the same Southern states that resisted the abolition of slavery during the Civil War. But most whites did not band together to right the wrongs caused by slavery, racial oppression, and organized bigotry. They ignored it as "not my problem."

The civil rights movement of the 1960s started as a religious crusade turned political, with blacks looking to the government to solve the problems of racism and oppression. Our federal, state, and local governments have, under pressure, instituted a variety of programs to fix the problems. (The recent Congress, unfortunately, has cut back many of these programs.) Continuing dialogue and some educational efforts to help people develop a sensitivity to different races and cultures seem only to result in the filing of more and more racism and discrimination cases. There continue to be ugly breakouts of racial tension, violence, and intolerance.

THE MELTING POT IS BOILING

The acclaimed melting pot of ethnic diversity in America has turned into a boiling cauldron of racial hostility and violence. Both blacks and whites continue to be guilty of prejudging, of seeing the other race and culture with a distorted view of reality. Many whites believe the stereotype of black men and women as dumb, resourceless, lazy, violent, and criminal. They see the black race as inferior to the white race. Many blacks, because of the past sins of slavery and the present attitudes of racism and oppression, distrust whites, some even developing a hatred toward whites.

Many decisions and policies on the federal, state, and local levels are based on race alone. Many white educators, government officials, and businessmen are prejudging as they go about their work of teaching, lobbying, buying, and selling. Many black students and would-be productive citizens *believed* the lie of the "inferiority" myth passed down from generation to generation and concluded that they cannot learn, cannot function in this society. So they gave up, do nothing, find trouble. Their true identity has been lost in negatives. Their purpose in life is shrouded by the cloud of racism.

I believe that almost every major issue that affects the well-being and future of America is centered around race. On every front, blacks and whites are poised for the ultimate race war. The volcano of race relations rumbles in the night, warning of another deadly eruption. If we allow it to erupt again by doing nothing, the white-hot lava of rage and violence will destroy families and communities—possibly the nation.

What is needed to eradicate the evils of racism is plenty of education along with the political and legislative actions. But they alone *cannot* bring about long-term change. I must point out that whenever a person tries to apply political answers to spiritual problems, the result is frustration. Spiritual problems deserve spiritual answers. Racism is a problem of the church. While government action is vital to begin the eradication of racism, only the healing of a person's heart can bring about long-term change. Only the saving and transforming power of Christ can ultimately change the racist's heart. The power of the Holy Spirit can purge the spiritual roots of racism from our society.

Unfortunately, even the church of Jesus Christ has been infected. Racist attitudes have inched their way into the very heart of the church, splitting it into two camps. Although many white Christians have confessed and repented of their racist and oppressive ways, many others continue to harbor attitudes of racism and hatred. Many white Christians believe that they are inherently superior to blacks and won't take advantage of what they could learn about God and the Bible from black ministers and teachers. There is a similar split among blacks. While many black Christians have confessed and repented of their distrust and anger toward whites, many others seethe at the sight or mention of white America and are suspicious (often rightly so) of most white theologians' interpretations of Scripture.

Racism is alive and well in the church because church members did not speak out and put this immorality to death long ago. Many white ministers through the years of Sunday mornings failed to preach against slavery back then and against racism now. They were silent, in effect taking the Fifth Amendment.

It is a tremendous tragedy that the church, particularly the white church, has been and continues to be one of the strongest institutions of racism. American churches (white churches actively and black churches passively) have participated in one of the most diabolical plots that now has paralyzed the body of Christ. The church, the institution of God's amazing grace and love whose foundation is to heal the hurts of humanity, has itself been hurt by attitudes of racial hatred and hostility. The consequences are widespread and deadly—racial tension, hostility, rage, violence, and civil unrest. Just look around you. Read your newspaper. Watch the TV news.

Because these issues were not dealt with in local churches or at the parent bodies of denominations, racism is alive and well. The effects are being felt throughout the body of Christ today. Does the church care? Consider the fact that many black and white Christians merely tolerate each other. There is no genuine desire or effort, on either side, to bring about racial reconciliation. Open the doors of any church on Sunday morning and you'll see that color barriers remain very real. Thus the body of Christ is strained. The cancers of racism and oppression are decaying the church and limiting its effectiveness in reaching the world for Christ.

RACISM IS ON GOD'S AGENDA

The Holy Spirit now is bringing this issue to the forefront. Just look at the recent "Memphis Miracle," where white Pentecostal denominations, in a meeting with black Pentecostal denominations, repented for preaching racism and for discriminatory actions against blacks for more than eighty years. Look at the Southern Baptist Convention, the largest Protestant denomination that has admitted that racism and discrimination against blacks were part of the foundation when the denomination was established. They also started some initial steps of repentance for these ungodly practices and policies. Even in the secular world—the recent O. J. Simpson trial and the Million-Man March on Washington, D.C.—racism has carved a place for heated discussions in every American's camp. Even in the state of Mississippi, where slavery was still legally on the books in 1995, there has been change. Legislation was introduced and passed abolishing slavery in the state.

Purging racism from the church, I believe, is one of the issues at the top of God's agenda today. We must not be spineless and hypocritical as leaders. We must take a stand and openly fight the war of racism nationally, locally, and personally, for it becomes a very personal issue.

The church, which has long been afraid to face the truth that racism exists in our congregations, must take up the cause and spread God's truth. Although there is controversy and confrontation associated with these changes, the Holy Spirit promises freedom, release, and a visitation to all who will accept and adhere to the illumination of these truths.

Chapter 3

God Gives Man Identity

The original Constitution of our country states that black people (because they were slaves) were counted as only three-fifths human.

The "God-fearing" men who wrote the Constitution must not have read the same Bible I read. Or maybe they tore certain pages out. Here is what the Word of God says:

> God said, "Let Us make man in Our image, according to Our likeness; let them have dominion over the fish of the sea, over the birds of the air, and over the cattle, over all the earth and over every creeping thing that creeps on the earth."
>
> So God created man in His own image; in the image of God He created him; male and female He created them.
>
> Then God blessed them, and God said to them, "Be fruitful and multiply; fill the earth and subdue it; have dominion over the fish of the sea, over the birds of the air, and over every living thing that moves on the earth." (Genesis 1:26–28 NKJV)

These verses are the basis and foundation for our identity. God gives humanity—including all the different races—identity. That means that he gives the black race, specifically, identity. We can say proudly that we are created in the *image* and *likeness* of God. The fact that we don't all look exactly alike doesn't matter. The fact that the color of our skin and hair is not all alike doesn't matter. We're not carbon copies. But we are all created in the *image* of God.

The Bible is perfectly clear to point out that *all* races are included in God's human family, and thus *all* are objects of his love. For black Christians and non-Christians alike, this is a truth that should liberate, emancipate, and swing open the prison gates of inferiority and self-hatred. We are not animals, creeping on the earth to be dominated. We are not three-fifths human, as the First Continental Congress chose to count black people because they were slaves, not free, thereby canceling us out of the rights spelled out for everyone else in the Constitution of the United States. No, we are uniquely crafted by the very hand of God, for he created *all* in his image and likeness. The same. Equal.

This equality is not based on standards set by white people, but on the standard of the Word of God. The Bible says that we were created in God's image, and he said his creation was good. The Bible also says that we are "fearfully and wonderfully made." God said it. I believe it. That settles it. No discussion. No debate. The case is closed.

Not only did God create us in his image and likeness, but we were instructed to be fruitful, to multiply, and to fill the earth and subdue it. He also has dominion over the fish of the sea, the birds of the air, and every living thing that moves on the earth. Something needs to be made clear at this point. Neither I nor any of my black brothers and sisters is a fish of the sea nor a bird of the air, and we definitely do not creep on four legs. God never commanded nor gave any person the right to rule over, enslave, control, or oppress another person.

You must understand that the desire to enslave and control people is the same whether it is in the spirit of colonialism, racism, or oppression or in the spirit of religion. This desire is one attitude that comes in many forms.

God created our inner and outer beings and knitted us together in our mother's womb. We should give him praise because we are fearfully and wonderfully made. Those who attempt to ridicule or oppress me because of the color of my skin, the shape of my nose, and the curliness of my hair are ridiculing not me, but the One who made me.

SEEING OURSELVES AS EQUAL

If there is ever to be unity and reconciliation among the races, white people must see black people as equal, but more importantly, black people must see themselves as equal. To reach that ideal, we must first understand the reality of today and yesterday, the reality that there are differences, the reality of a false "standard." Whites have been taught that they are the standard, and that blacks and the rest of the world must meet that standard. Look at a few simple illustrations of this "standard." You've heard of "flesh-colored" nylons or pantyhose, even Band-Aids. My question—whose flesh? Or consider the language and speaking style in the United States. Turn on the nightly news and listen to the similarities of voice, of wording, of pronunciation—all adhering to the white standard. Think back not too many years to the black women who began straightening their hair to look more like white women. These are just a few examples of how white people have become the standard by which all others are judged. This is wrong and prejudicial, discriminatory and racist.

Whites have been taught that they are superior; blacks have been taught that they are inferior. Achievement tests used in the schools of today are used to prove that lie. There also are the studies that conclude in scientific-sounding wording that there is a basic difference in learning ability between the black and white races, as if there were different origins, ignoring all the other factors that relate to education and learning. Another lie! We were all created in the image and likeness of God. We all have the same *character* of God. He did not create one race to be superior to another race.

What is needed now is for us all—all races—to see each other as equal. Only then will we be ready to start the much-needed reconciliation process between the races and between individuals.

Part 2

Denied Our True Identity

Chapter 4

Satan Distorts Man's Identity

What happened to our identity? Why are we groping in darkness, ignorant of who we are? The character that we call Satan happened. He has blinded our eyes to our true identity—created in the image and likeness of God.

Satan was a high-ranking archangel, responsible for one-third of the angels and for the praise and worship of God. The worship experience must have felt good to him, because he wanted rule and dominion that was not his. He proclaimed: "I will be like the Most High God, I will exalt my throne above the throne of God."

He even influenced one-third of the angels in heaven to rebel against God, but his bid for power in heaven failed. Since he couldn't get to rule in the heavens, he came to earth to try to achieve his purposes.

The Bible says, "Woe to the inhabitants of the earth and the sea! For the devil has come down to you, having great wrath, because he knows that he has a short time" (Revelation 12:12 NKJV).

Satan (also called Lucifer) is an eternally unemployed choir director who has a messiah complex. He has an obsession for ruling, even though God has not given him authority to rule. Those who desire illegal rule and dominion over others become akin to Satan.

> Now the serpent was more cunning than any beast of the field which the LORD God had made. And he said to the woman, "Has God indeed said, 'You shall not eat of every tree of the garden'?"
> And the woman said to the serpent, "We may eat the fruit of the trees of the garden; but of the fruit of the tree which is in the midst of the garden, God has said, 'You shall not eat it, nor shall you touch it, lest you die.'"
> And the serpent said to the woman, "You will not surely die. For God knows that in the day you eat of it your eyes will be opened, and *you will be like God*, knowing good and evil." (Gen. 3:1–5 NKJV, emphasis added)

In this passage Satan begins to distort the identity of man by distorting the Word of God. The snare is "and you will be like God." God had already said that Adam and Eve were like God, "created in the image and likeness of God." Satan's saying, "If you eat of this tree of the knowledge of good and evil you will be like God," implies that they were not quite like God yet, and that God was in some way holding out on them. His bait was that they would "be like God." His attack was against their *identity* and their association or connection with God. He wanted them to believe that God had lied to them. They listened to Satan and ate of the tree, disobeying God's Word. As a result of Satan's scheme and their disobedience, they lost both the place that God had given them and their dominion on the earth.

From the moment that this unemployed choir director heard "be fruitful and multiply; fill the earth and subdue it. Have dominion over the fish of the sea, over the birds of the air, and over every living thing that moves on the earth," he desired this rule, this dominion. By assaulting the identity of man, Satan got illegal rule and dominion on earth. He got the dominion over the earth that God had given to man.

The evil of illegal rule, unjust dominion, and enslavement of other human beings begins in the heart of the oppressor and is played out by distorting the enslaveds' identity and, most of all, their view of God. In the same way, our identity as a black race was assaulted first by white missionaries and then by colonialists so they could gain control. That control has continued right through the years of slavery and, for too many blacks, right up until today.

A DISTORTED IMAGE

The only way that you can gain control of others, making them believe that they are somehow inferior, is to distort their image of God or to give them a wrong God. Our people were labeled "heathens" by the early missionaries and considered "inferior." Our people didn't meet the standards of these whites. They said our hair was wrong, our nose was wrong, our lips were wrong, our walk was wrong, and the way we worshiped God was wrong. They assaulted our identity and who we were. In fact, they gave us another

God, one they said didn't like our hair, our nose, our lips, our way of singing, our dance, or our beat.

The religious world and its ambassadors started this distortion of how God created us and ultimately how we see ourselves. Religion is still distorting our image, our identity. Too many blacks still worship that God given to us by the colonialists, a God of laws. This philosophy has us working religious formulas, trying to *earn* our salvation by works, ignoring the true Word of God that offers us salvation through Jesus Christ, not by works. My Bible says that I am a king, a priest, a chosen generation, a royal priesthood, a holy nation. The Scriptures say I am a saint! I am justified! This salvation-by-works philosophy has us trying to take just one more catechism class, or praying one more time, in order to be acceptable to God. And being black, we have to work even harder than whites.

But the Almighty God likes our hair, our nose, our lips, our way of singing because he made us the way we are, and he said, "It is good." I am here to proclaim as loudly as I possibly can and to all who will listen: We don't have to pray one more prayer, read one more book, or sing one more song in order to be what we already are—accepted by God.

Chapter 5

Man Distorts Man's Identity

Satan played a major role in distorting man's identity and has continued to influence others to do the same. He uses humanly influenced religion and philosophy and even those with so-called good intentions to do his work.

No matter what the philosophy—whether Muslim, Hindu, Humanism, Intellectualism, or even a distorted view of Christianity—and no matter how different one is from another, they all have one characteristic in common: They never exalt man. They debase and undermine man's identity, reducing man to a level lower than where the Lord placed him.

The **Hindu religion** sees man as an insignificant part of the whole ethos of life. Man is no different from a dog or a bird. The Hindus allow their people to starve by the thousands, while cows roam freely in the fields. They see cows as something sacred and related to God, never as food for their people. People are seen as less than a cow. If my family and I lived in India, I'd play a religious role in the daytime and say, "Yeah, cow, I worship you, cow." But at night my family and I would go "shopping," and we'd find us some beef. In the morning, I'd be picking my teeth.

One of the beliefs behind the reincarnation theory of the Hindu religion is that everybody and everything has the chance to upgrade or downgrade the status of his/her existence after death, based on his/her present life. If you are good in the present life, then you might be reincarnated ("born again") as a Brahman, a lighter-skinned Indian with a higher class or status. But if you are bad in this life, you have the dismal assurance that you will be reincarnated as something with a lower class or status, like a camel, driven by people. Animals have the same chance as human beings to upgrade to someone or something of higher class or status. Thus there is no real distinction between human beings and animals.

The **heathen cultures,** those who have no religion or have many gods, distort man's view of God by seeing man as a part of the system of Nature. They see God as the wind, the rain, or the sun. If God is the wind, then I am viewed as just a breeze. If God is the rain, then I am viewed as just a drop. And if God is the sun, then I am viewed as just a ray. When man's view of God is distorted, then his view of humanity becomes distorted.

Humanists destroy and distort man's view of God by saying man can be God without God. Humanism believes that man is the ultimate standard for living. Furthermore, all important decisions in life are relative to each situation. There are no moral absolutes. If this is true, then there is no Almighty Creator of the Universe and no heavenly Father of Creation. This philosophy is wrong. Man is not God within himself. The ultimate result of humanism is destruction. "There is a way which seemeth right unto a man, but the end thereof are the ways of death" (Proverbs 14:12; 16:25).

Spiritualism distorts man's image or view of God by seeing man as an immature spirit encumbered by a body. Man as a spiritualist needs more mature spirits to guide him. This philosophy is a strong force behind the New Age Movement that had its beginnings in transcendental meditation and metaphysics and became very popular in the United States in the 1970s.

But the sinker of them all is the distorted view of **Christianity** given to Africans by many white missionaries, continued through the years of slavery, and still preached in some churches today.

Instead of true Christianity, we got a type of religion that subdued us and oppressed us and said that we were cursed. We were brought under the slave masters' whips—supposedly God-fearing slave masters, Bible-totin' slave masters who went to church, who prayed to God, but were beating us and killing us, selling us like cattle.

It's no wonder that black people looked elsewhere—to the Muslim movement, Obeah, Voodoo, ancestral spirits, and the worship of animals and the elements. They were trying to find some relief from what whites called Christianity. Christianity as presented by whites had been warped and distorted. It had become an enemy to black people.

The white missionaries and colonialists gave us a God who sanctioned slavery and oppression. The colonialists exploited us economically and raped our lands, our history, our culture, our women. The most unfortunate commentary to be made is that these people professed to be religious and conquered other lands and other peoples in the name of religion. They gave us a blond-haired, blue-eyed image of Jesus as our Savior. That's not biblical. Have you ever seen a Hebrew who has blond hair and blue eyes? And Jesus was Hebrew, a Jew. Do you want to know who was the "model" for that famous painting of Jesus done by Michelangelo during the Renaissance period? None other than Michelangelo's uncle. I believe this was done for identification for whites and to promote, however subtly, a sense of superiority among whites, and inferiority among blacks. But God said no images (See Exodus 20:4)!

To have any chance of being accepted, the conquered Africans had to take on a new identity, becoming like the British. They had to talk like the British and act like them. They were fed European history while being denied their own history, heritage, and culture. They were manipulated into feeling inferior and believing they needed white people to survive. Once a person believes that he is less than you are and that you are superior, you can control and oppress him, make him your slave.

The church in America became an instrument to keep the slaves docile, accepting of their fate as slaves. In the early 1800s, blacks in this country could not worship in the same sanctuaries as whites. At least not in the Methodist church. Blacks had to sit outside the windows or in the loft. In places where slaves were allowed to attend worship services, the God they heard about was the wrong God, a God used to keep them in line by promising salvation in the hereafter for those who obeyed their masters.

One black got tired of that kind of treatment and formed a new denomination, the African Methodist Episcopal (AME) Church, dedicated to the principle of black people worshiping freely. His name was Richard Allen. The AME was organized on April 9, 1816.

We think that the government of a country protects the rights of all who live within its borders. But the men in the first American government, set up after the Revolutionary War, did nothing to stop slavery in the new nation. They did ban the importing of slaves, but not for twenty years. And during those twenty years, they even levied an import tax on each new slave brought into the country, thereby profiting from the evil.

But the wording in the Constitution of the United States, dating back to 1787, that stung the most and is remembered the longest, right to today, is counting slaves, for purposes of taxation and representation, as only "three-fifths of a person." Slaves were property, and the men who wrote the Constitution believed in protecting property— for the owners. To provide moral justification for those who owned slaves, the religious community spread as "truth" that blacks had no souls, another lie remembered with pain to this day.

The Emancipation Proclamation that President Abraham Lincoln signed during the Civil War, in 1863, freed more than four million black men, women, and children, but didn't free all the slaves. It didn't take a moral stand against slavery. It was a military tactic designed to help the North defeat the South. Lincoln freed only slaves in the states that had withdrawn from the Union. Slaves in Northern states remained in servitude. It would be another two years before the United States, with ratification of the Thirteenth Amendment to the Constitution, finally abolished slavery.

The Fourteenth Amendment, passed in 1868, guaranteed freedom for all and equal protection under the law. The Fifteenth Amendment, in 1870, gave voting rights to black men. (Women—black and white—didn't get to vote until 1920 with ratification by the states of the Nineteenth Amendment.)

Continuing its role of protector of human rights, the Congress, in 1875, passed the Civil Rights Bill, which became the basis for the civil rights movement almost a century later. It states:

> All persons within the jurisdiction of the United States shall be entitled to the full and equal enjoyment of the accommodations, advantages, facilities, and privileges of inns, public conveyances on land or water, theaters, and other places of public amusement; subject only to the conditions and limitations established by law and applicable alike to citizens of every race and color, regardless of any previous condition of servitude.

Sounds good, doesn't it? But it took almost a hundred years and a lot of marches, sit-ins, and prayer vigils and finally a feisty black woman named Rosa Parks on a public bus to begin any real change, to tear down the "Colored" signs above water fountains and rest rooms, to open the front seats of public buses to blacks, to open the doors of all schools to students, regardless of the color of their skin.

Where was the church during all this change? All too silent or preaching the wrong message. Let's focus on the racism against blacks that is still so pervasive, especially in the church. As blacks, we can now eat dinner in a restaurant seated next to tables occupied by whites. We can sign in to the fanciest hotel in town. But even today, many whites in general and Christians in particular continue to harbor attitudes of racism and oppression toward blacks. They continue to see us as inferior human beings, some even considering us less than human.

It comes down to a person's relationship with God. If a person does not see God correctly, that person will never see me correctly. If a person's image of God is incorrect, that person's image of who I am will be incorrect.

Some well-meaning whites say to black people, "When I see you, I don't see you as black." They think they are giving us a compliment.

But I ask, "Why don't you see me as black? Are you blind? I am black." It seems as if they see my blackness as some disease that they are willing to overlook. But my blackness—our blackness—is as much a part of our identity as our height, our eyes, and our hair. When someone says that they don't see us as black, they are denying our identity and essentially who we are.

Whenever that happens, we must remember that what matters most is not what others think of us but how God sees us and what he thinks of us.

Part 3

Our Identity and Our Purpose

Chapter 6

Tracing Our Biblical Roots

You should not let truth and information that is being shared make you bitter. You should let truth make you better.

How did we as blacks lose our heritage? How did we become separated from God?

First, we need to know that blacks were very involved in early Bible days. In fact, the first eleven chapters of the Bible deal with world history that includes black history, not just Jewish history. God had no problem with color of skin. He created it. He just didn't put any emphasis on it.

So why should we emphasize it now? There are those who say that color doesn't matter. They say, if we are born again, if we are Christians, if we know Christ, why do we have to emphasize blacks in the Bible? If we are serving God, we should love one another, we should meet together, and it doesn't matter what color we are.

But you have to remember the principle of Scripture: first the natural, and then the spiritual. The thirty-nine books in the Old Testament are a foundation for the natural.

They bring forth the twenty-seven books in the New Testament, in the spiritual. The Old Testament is established on all the truths that actually happened in history. The books of the New Testament deal with the truth based on the New Covenant, established on what happened in those other thirty-nine books. There is a saying: "The New is in the Old contained, while the Old is in the New explained. The New is in the Old concealed, while the Old is in the New revealed." So all the spiritual truths that make up the New Covenant, that we are part of as Christians, were established on Old Testament reality. First the natural, then the spiritual. And it is important to know the natural.

Another argument is that there is no need for emphasizing "natural ethnicity," for emphasizing blacks in the Bible, because there is no Jew nor Gentile, no bond nor free. Think about it. No Jew nor Gentile; no race distinction. No bond nor free. That means no class distinction. There is no Barbarian. No Scythian. No cultural distinction. No male or female. No sexual distinction. No circumcised nor uncircumcised. No denominational distinction.

THE DIFFERENCES ARE REAL

In Christ, or in the Anointed One—or what I call "in the action of the Anointed One or in the anointing"—there is no racial, no sexual, no class, no cultural, or denominational distinction. But in practice, in daily living, there is a difference. We don't stop being a male or a female because we are Christians. We don't say, "You are no longer a male or a female because you are in Christ, so forget all of those natural things."

We also know that there is but one church in Christ. But in practice, in daily living, there is the Baptist Church, the Methodist, Episcopal, Pentecostal, Charismatic, and on and on. All of these continue in daily life, in practice. In Christ, there is no distinction. That is in the anointing. But in our daily life, even though we are all progressively coming into Christ, we still live in the natural, and there is a distinction.

In this country, this nation, we label the people of this country "Americans" as an identity, as being a part of one nation. But under the notion that there is no difference in this world, we'd have to say, don't call us Americans, just say we are all of the human race. There is no difference. Don't say you are from Missouri; say you are part of the human race.

But there are differences—subgroups in the big group. We are all part of the human race, living on earth. Some of us are Americans. Some of us are Americans and from Missouri. And some of us are Americans, from Missouri—and black. There are differences. In people. In nations. We all have different locations, or habitations. Different cultures, races, geographical boundaries. And the Word of God must be preached to all, right down to the country, the city, the family, and to the individual. To every "nation." The word *nation* in Matthew 24:14 means to every *race*. The Greek word there is *ethnos*. It's where we get the English phrase *ethnic group*. So the Gospel is to go to every race. There is a difference.

God will specifically visit and deal with different ethnic groups, deal with their different problems. That is why you can find revival in one nation in Africa, while another nation is doing nothing. The same is happening in Asia and Europe. And in the Americas, and in the United States. Because God chooses in his own time to deal with different ethnic groups.

EACH ONE HAS A HISTORY

Linked to those different nations, or races, is the history of each. If history is not important, then why did God give the Jewish people, the Hebrew people, thousands of years of chronological history? He gave them all those years of history so they'd be strong enough as a nation to birth the Messiah. And strong enough, through a rich sense of heritage about themselves and their history, to survive all the persecution that Jewish people have come under.

I once heard a German lady say to a Jewish talk show host, "Why do you keep bringing up all this talk about the Holocaust? Why do you keep bringing up the things that happened to the Jews? That happened in the past and we do not want to hear it anymore."

The Jewish talk show host became angry. "Don't you bring that kind of attitude to us. We must tell our history. We must tell it over and over again *so it doesn't happen again!*"

If you don't understand your history, you are bound to repeat it. History brings a sense of heritage, a sense of being, a sense of purpose. We learn from our history, whether it is the history of last month and an important lesson learned, or the history of ancestors and what they knew.

The main focus in the Bible is the history of the Hebrews and everything they did as it related to God. Why? Because God chose the Hebrews. "He will set you high above all nations which He has made, in praise, in name, and in honor, and that you may be a holy people to the LORD your God, just as He has spoken" (Deuteronomy 26:19 NKJV). And it was through the Hebrews that God chose to work to reach every other race.

"And ye shall know the truth and the truth shall make you free" (John 8:32). We must see that as a people we have been a part of God's revelation of himself to man. The record of the Bible, especially the Old Testament, is really a historical record. We were very much a part of God's revelation to man from the very beginning of creation, in the Scriptures as well as in secular history. In fact, our ancestral home, and our ancestral people are mentioned in relation to the Garden of Eden. Two of the rivers mentioned in the Garden of Eden were definitely related to lands where black people dwelt. One was named Pishon (the Nile), which went to the land of Havilah, or Egypt. That is a land of black people. Here is where most of what we call Africa originated (see Genesis 2:10). Another river, the Gihon, wound through the land of Cush, which means "black."

A black priest named Melchizedek blessed Abraham, who is the father of the Hebrew race. Melchizedek was the king of Salem, the ancient city of Jerusalem, and a priest of the Most High God.

NATIONS OF COLOR

Actually, on the Day of Pentecost (Acts 2:10), of the sixteen nations that were there, almost all were nations of color. They were either from Africa or from other areas where the people were dark-skinned. Two nations were specifically from Africa—Egypt and Libya (see Acts 2:9–11). Think of that! We as black people were right there!

In Acts 1:8, Jesus said, "But ye shall receive power, after that the Holy Ghost is come upon you: and ye shall be witnesses unto me both in Jerusalem, and in all Judaea, and in Samaria, and unto the uttermost part of the earth." Then the disciples were scattered abroad everywhere to preach Christ.

The first Gentile that God used to extend the Gospel beyond the area of Israel was the Ethiopian eunuch. Remember, Philip was told to go down to Samaria. And in the last part of Acts 8, he sees the Ethiopian eunuch, who had been to Jerusalem and was returning home. Philip is told to go to him, to talk to him. The eunuch's name was Endich, and he became the bishop of the first church of Ethiopia. So the first fully Gentile nation that began to establish Christianity was Ethiopia, a black African nation. And the men of Cyprus and Cyrene, a people of color, took the Gospel from Jerusalem as far as Antioch.

Antioch, a missionary church concerned for the rest of the body of Christ, became a pattern of the perfect church. The Antioch church had not only Jewish but black leadership. In fact, there were prophets and teachers there who were black. There was Simeon, who was called Niger, and Lucius of Cyrene, a city in the northern African nation of Libya. Both were black. Niger is a river in Africa and the name of an African nation. Actually, the word Niger means "of the black origin." And Saul and Barnabas and Manaen (who grew up with Herod the tetrarch) were there at the Antioch church (Acts 13:1).

They were fasting before the Lord in a prophetic presbytery service, and the Holy Spirit said, "Separate me Barn-

abas and Saul for the work whereunto I have called them"
(Acts 13:2). So these other three laid hands on Saul (who
became Paul) and Barnabas and ordained them, and commissioned them, imparting to them what they needed to go
out and fulfill their call.

Imagine, two of the three men who laid hands on Paul,
the man who wrote most of the New Testament, were black.

In Paul's accolades in Romans 16, he writes, asking the
Romans to greet Rufus and his mother (Romans 16:13).
Rufus was the son of Simon, who helped Jesus carry the
cross. Simon's sons, Alexander and Rufus, were a part of
the church leadership. So Paul claimed Rufus, a black man,
as his "brother." He claimed Rufus's mother as his
"mother." Paul must have gone over to Rufus's house and
had some greens and cornbread, because Paul felt he had
been treated like a son. Paul called Rufus and Lucius, who
was one of the prophets participating in Paul's ordination,
"kinsmen."

Even though blacks were very much a part of the early
church, that's not the truth we've been told. We don't see
"black" when we imagine Bible scenes. We think that all
the people of the Bible were white or Roman—because
that's how white illustrators and painters have depicted the
scenes from those days.

They didn't do their research. If they had, the pictures
we look at would have been quite different. The only
whites during Paul's day were Romans and Greeks. All the
other nations that were named—Medes and Parthians, for
example—were all people of color. And when you follow
church history, and study the lives of the church fathers,
you find that many of them were people of color.

IDENTITY LOST

But if blacks were there at the beginning of the New Testament church and in the Old Testament, what happened? Why don't we know that? We got lost in the translations, and in the Dark Ages. We as a people were lost in history. Overlooked. Because of this deletion of our historic part in early Christianity, blacks, not unlike the Jews of Moses' time, eventually turned to other forms of worship. Many became Muslims, following the teachings of Muhammad. Others sought solace and guidance from what we call "heathen" religions. They turned to animism, trying to find some element of strength in the natural world around them. Some chose the worship of animals; others looked toward ancestral spirits, seeking help and comfort by trying to revive their ancestors.

Blacks and other people of color weren't the only ones who were lost. The Dark Ages, in fact, was a period when there was great apostasy, a falling away. During that time, evil was reigning, and there were witches, warlocks, plagues, and sickness. The true church somehow got stymied. The European nations developed during the Dark Ages, though it would be some time before they would become strong. When Constantine, the Emperor of the Roman Empire, was converted to Christianity, Christianity became popular.

Christianity basically had stayed pure under the persecution by systems of the world. The persecution seemed to keep Christians separate, set apart from the world. But when the church joined with the world, there was a merging of philosophy and religion, and we got theology. We got interpretations of the Bible by men. We got abuse through those interpretations. Leaders began to use the

Bible for selfish means, as a tool to control the people. The Roman Catholic Church evolved during this time. Then came the Protestant movement, a protest against what had happened to the church, led by Martin Luther.

About this time the slavery market started. Some of the people involved in capturing slaves and in the buying and selling of slaves were a part of this new Christianity, this religion that was a tool of oppression and not of freedom. Whites used Christianity to endorse slavery and the oppression of people.

We as a people were finally separated from our ancestors and our history by slavery. We talk of the Holocaust and the six million Jews who were killed during World War II. We talk of it so that it will never happen again. We don't talk about the millions of blacks who died in the Atlantic Ocean, died when slave ships went down in storms, or died when they were cast overboard still chained together to hide illegal trafficking in human cargo. These blacks never got to the Americas or to the islands in the Caribbean. They were lost on the way.

It is essential to know who we are as a people. It is essential to know our religious history all the way back to early Bible days. We lost our connection with Africa, and the land of creation, and the land where the Garden of Eden was, and the land where our ancestors walked with God and were a part of the revelation of God to man.

LIVING IN VIOLENCE

You might ask, if blacks did so much in the past, during Bible days, what has happened to blacks today? Why is there so much violence? Why? We are a product of the violence we have been under. We were brought to this country under violence, suppressed under violence, kept in check under violence, and now are being regulated by violence, by the police brutality that is a way of life in black neighborhoods. When you live with violence all the time, you produce seed after your own kind. You breed violence.

But in the midst of all this violence, perhaps because of it, there now is a tremendous visitation and revival happening in a segment of the black church. The fastest growing church movement in America today is in the Independent Pentecostal and Charismatic churches in the black and Hispanic segments of the church, especially in the South but now even in the East.

And the focus is a strong emphasis on the Word, teaching the reality of who we are in Scripture, and knowing Christ as our "liberator," knowing our culture and heritage. That is why it is important for us as a people to put black people back into the scenes of the Bible. That's why it is important to see the truth of our history.

This revival has brought a new thrust, the likes of which have not been seen since the Azusa Street movement of 1906. This revival hasn't yet reached the young people. God started by revealing the truth about our identity and our heritage in Scripture. That is the first process. To be free you must restore your identity.

The Lord says in Psalm 72 that in his due time, he will deliver the needy and the poor and will break the back of the oppressor. All these Scriptures are coming alive because God is trying to raise us back up, to get us connected back to our beginning, to our heritage.

We are beginning to know what blacks have done in relation to God. We are beginning to know how blacks walked with God and how they were a part of God's plan. This restoration helps to bring a sense of direction, a sense of purpose, a sense of identity that stops all the madness.

Chapter 7

Jesus and the Issue of Identity

It is always dangerous to live under an oppressive system. You can at any time become a threat to the power structure. So you have to be careful, keep your "place," keep your mouth shut, not rile anyone, remain unnoticed. Or something bad could happen. Those in power must define your identity in such a way that benefits them and keeps their power secure and you submissive, compliant.

One of the biggest issues that Jesus had to deal with while on earth was his identity. His was not a problem of *not* knowing who he was. He got into trouble because he knew who he was and from whom he had come. And why.

Jesus Christ can identify with blacks of today because he, too, lived under an oppressive system. He lived in the Roman Empire, which controlled his culture, his race, his history, and his religion. But Jesus was not intimidated by the cultural or religious power structures of that day. He didn't stay in his "place." He didn't keep his mouth shut. And he certainly didn't remain unnoticed. He riled many.

The religious power structure (scribes, Pharisees, chief priests, and so forth) joined with the civil power structure (King Herod, for one) and the worldly power structure (Pilate) in order to silence the One who knew who he was. Yet Jesus boldly proclaimed his true identity despite strong pressure (even the threat of peril) to deny his identity.

Listen to the Master: "And Jesus said unto them, I am the bread of life: he that cometh to me shall never hunger; and he that believeth on me shall never thirst" (John 6:35).

He didn't stutter or stammer. Jesus boldly and uncompromisingly declared who he was to the religious leaders of that day. But they didn't believe him. They were not accustomed to "a nobody" speaking with such boldness and assurance. Listen to their response to his declaration: "The Jews then murmured at him, because he said, I am the bread which came down from heaven" (John 6:41). They got upset and murmured because Jesus boldly proclaimed who he was. They didn't murmur at what he *did*, but at who he said he *was*. His sense of identity upset the Jewish leaders because they wouldn't believe him. He didn't fit their idea of a Messiah, a king of the Jews. So they sent guards to arrest him.

Despite the threats, he continued to proclaim who he was:

I am that bread of life. Your fathers did eat manna in the wilderness, and are dead. This is the bread which cometh down from heaven, that man may eat thereof, and not die. I am the living bread which came down from heaven: if any man eat of this bread, he shall live for ever; and the bread that I will give is my flesh, which I will give for the life of the world. (John 6:48–51)

He was confident in his declaration because he was confident in who he was. He didn't shuffle his feet, shrug his shoulders, or hang his head, because he knew his identity, his purpose, his destiny.

When he expressed who he was, the Jews argued with one another. "The Jews therefore strove among themselves" (John 6:52). The conversation may have gone something like this: "Did you hear what he said? He said he was the living bread." Another responds, "No, he didn't. You misunderstood him." "I know what I heard. He said, 'If you eat My flesh, you'll live forever.'" The other responds again, "He didn't say that. You're exaggerating and taking his words out of context." There was much controversy among the crowd because of the truth of who Jesus was, a truth the crowd didn't recognize, didn't believe.

In verses 53–56 of John, chapter 6, Jesus declares more intently who he is: "Except ye eat the flesh of the Son of man, and drink his blood, ye have no life in you. Whoso eateth my flesh, and drinketh my blood, hath eternal life." Many of his followers were horrified by the literal meaning of the words. "This is an hard saying; who can hear it?" (John 6:60). Jesus responded to his followers after they murmured about what he had said: "When Jesus knew in himself that his disciples murmured about it, he said to them, 'Doth this offend you?'" (John 6:61). Jesus knew that what he said offended them. He asked them the question to let them know that he knew what was in their hearts. In other words, he said, "I know that what I've said about my identity offends you, but I need to ask you so I can hear from your mouths that you are offended." Jesus knew that there were some who did not believe.

In so many words Jesus was saying, "If you are offended, you are getting offended because I am speaking words that are spirit and words that are life" (John 6:63–64, author's translation). After Jesus spoke, many who had been followers left him (John 6:66). They couldn't hang with Jesus anymore because he knew his identity, his purpose, and his destiny, and they couldn't accept his identity.

DECLARING IDENTITY BRINGS DANGER

Jesus' declaration of identity caused much opposition and controversy. In John 10, Jesus declared who he was after he had healed a man who had been blind from birth. He continued to add to his declarations of who he was: "I am the door [gate] of the sheep" (John 10:7). Jesus continued to openly declare his identity: "I am the good shepherd: the good shepherd giveth his life for the sheep" (John 10:11). He continues a few verses later with the same declaration:

> I am the good shepherd, and know my sheep, and am known of mine. As the Father knoweth me, even so know I the Father: and I lay down my life for the sheep. And other sheep I have, which are not of this fold: them also I must bring, and they shall hear my voice; and there shall be one fold, and one shepherd. Therefore doth my Father love me, because I lay down my life, that I might take it again. No man taketh it from me, but I lay it down of myself. I have

power to lay it down, and I have power to take it again. This commandment have I received of my Father. (John 10:14–18)

Jesus made an absolutely bold and true declaration about himself and his identity. His declaring his identity split the Jews. "There was a division therefore again among the Jews for these sayings" (John 10:19). They were arguing because of who Jesus said he was. Jesus did not have a problem with who he was, but other people (scribes, Pharisees, and others) did.

In fact, after the Jews debated over Jesus' identity, he began to proclaim with more conviction who he was: "I and my Father are one" (John 10:30). I can imagine that his disciples were saying, "Please don't say that, Jesus. You're going to make the Jews angry. They're going to accuse you of blasphemy. You're going to get us killed."

Jesus continued to proclaim, "I and my Father are one." Don't say that! "I and my Father are one." Don't say that, please! "I and my Father are one!"

The Jews responded in a destructive way. They picked up stones to stone him (John 10:31). Jesus' declaration of his identity made the Jews so angry that they actually intended to do him bodily harm. He did not fit the traditional model or status quo of that day. Jesus, because he knew who he was and Whose he was, did not have the downcast or inferior mentality expected of him.

Jesus seemed to be surprised at the Jews' response. "Jesus answered them, Many good works have I shewed you from my Father; for which of those works do ye stone me?" (John 10:32). His response was, What have I done that has made you want to actually hurt me? What work made you so upset? What miracle was done out of order?

It wasn't what Jesus had done that got him into trouble. The crowd was ready to stone him because of his identity. "The Jews answered him, saying, For a good work we stone thee not; but for blasphemy; and because that thou, being a man, makest thyself God" (John 10:33). They did not want to stone him for what he did, but for *who he was*. His proclamation of his identity was the thing that upset the Jews and the religious world. He especially upset them because he associated his identity with *God himself*.

Jesus' identity and his link with deity upset the power structure, particularly the religious power structure.

> Jesus answered them, Is it not written in your law, I said, Ye are gods? If he called them gods, unto whom the word of God came, and the scripture cannot be broken; Say ye of him, whom the Father hath sanctified, and sent into the world, Thou blasphemest; because I said, I am the Son of God? If I do not the works of my Father, believe me not. But if I do, though ye believe not me, believe the works: that ye may know, and believe, that the Father *is* in me, and I in him. (John 10:34–38)

Jesus' proclamation of the truth, stating who he really was, put him in danger. "Therefore they sought again to take him: but he escaped out of their hand" (John 10:39).

When they asked Jesus, "Who are you?" he answered: "I am the way, the truth, and the life.... I am the Son of God. I am the good shepherd" (John 14:6; 10:36; 10:14).

The issue was, who *are* you? Listen to the Word of God:

> Then Pilate entered into the judgment hall again, and called Jesus, and said unto him, Art thou the King of the Jews? Jesus answered him, Sayest thou this thing of thyself, or did others tell it thee of me? Pilate answered, Am I a Jew? Thine own nation and the chief priests have delivered thee unto me: what hast thou done? Jesus answered, My kingdom is not of this world: if my kingdom were of this world, then would my servants fight, that I should not be delivered to the Jews: but now is my kingdom not from hence. Pilate therefore said unto him, Art thou a king then? Jesus answered, Thou sayest that I am a king. To this end was I born, and for this cause came I into the world, that I should bear witness unto the truth. Every one that is of the truth heareth my voice. Pilate saith unto him, What is truth? And when he had said this, he went out again unto the Jews, and saith unto them, I find in him no fault *at all*. (John 18:33–38)

The power structure of the world, evidenced through Pilate, and the religious power structure, evidenced through the chief priests, the Pharisees, and the scribes, were upset about who Jesus said he was. From their perspective, if he really was a king, he was a threat to their power. Those in power remained there by keeping people in their place, not by allowing anyone to become a leader of the masses. Yet Pilate would have released Jesus because of his own conscience and his wife's dream. But he gave in to the masses shouting: "Crucify him!"

And Pilate wrote a title, and put it on the cross. And the writing was, JESUS OF NAZARETH THE KING OF THE JEWS. This title then read many of the Jews: for the place where Jesus was crucified was nigh to the city: and it was written in Hebrew, and Greek, and Latin. Then said the chief priests of the Jews to Pilate, write not The King of the Jews; but that he said, I am King of the Jews. Pilate answered, What I have written I have written. (John 19:19–22)

According to the custom, the *crime* for which a man was crucified was to be written on a placard. But Pilate wrote on the placard who Jesus *was!* Because that was his crime—who he was! He was crucified not for what he did but for *who he was!* The chief priests (religious power structure) were upset by what Pilate wrote, which gave Jesus' true identity, because they didn't want his real identity to be entered into the permanent records.

PART OF GOD'S PURPOSE

Our true identity is linked to God. We all are created in the image and likeness of God. We all are a part of God's purpose.

Yet our true image was denied by slaveholders and those who sold our people into slavery. They said we were like animals. They housed us like animals. They treated us like animals, like property. The early government in America even counted black people as only three-fifths human. They said we had no soul. They denied us education and true spirituality. They denied us family. They denied our history. White people were legally free to enslave and oppress blacks.

Those who would keep black people oppressed cannot allow us to be linked with God, for through God comes strength and purpose. Power structures that want to keep you oppressed cannot allow you to link yourself to God, because they want to be God to you. They want to justify the enslaved position they have you in and how they treat you. Since the reality is that you are created in the image and likeness of God, and you are a part of God's purpose and plan, others have to accept you as an equal. They therefore cannot find any justification for your mal-treatment.

The church is the continuation of the manifestation of God in the flesh. Our human flesh or life is important because God wants to use us to manifest his glory (apparentness) and his will in the world. The foundation for the New Covenant is: "And the Word was made flesh, and dwelt [tabernacled] among us, (and we beheld his glory)" (John 1:14). If we truly are members of the body of Christ, it means that we share Christ's identity, not only in spirit, but also in the flesh.

Identity is important. God created us as a reflection of himself in the natural. We are made the way we are in order to fulfill God's purposes on the earth. God could have used many other means, but instead he chose to use human flesh, real live human beings to reveal himself and to accomplish his purposes.

It is my contention that since the majority of the people of the world are people of color, we must play a big role in fulfilling God's purposes on earth. We have a big role in reflecting who the Lord is by the way the Lord made us. God said:

> There is a place where someone has testified:
> "What is man that you are mindful of him,
>   the son of man that you care for him?
> You made him a little lower than the angels;
>   you crowned him with glory and honor
>   and put everything under his feet."
>
> In putting everything under him, God left nothing that is not subject to him. Yet at present we do not see everything subject to him. But we see Jesus, who was made a little lower than the angels, now crowned with glory and honor because he suffered death, so that by the grace of God he might taste death for everyone. (Hebrews 2:6–9 NIV)

God is very conscious of us, individually and as a people. Our humanity and the way he made us is important to him and to his purposes on the earth. Every day, by the Spirit, we are being conformed to the image of his Son.

When you deny who you are, you are actually denying the God who made you. When others attempt to deny your identity, they are attempting to deny your purpose in creation and your link to the image of God.

Jesus was manifested in the flesh to the Jews, who had a history with God, to fulfill the purposes of God on the earth. Jesus declared, "I know whence I came, and whither I go" (John 8:14). Jesus was manifested in the flesh to do the will of the Father. "For this purpose the Son of God was manifested [in the flesh], that he might destroy the works of the devil" (1 John 3:8).

Our manifestation in the flesh and in the natural also relates to God's purpose for us as a people on the earth. God has a purpose for us. We must remember that. But first we must keep our link to that purpose through Christ. Second, we must follow the example that Christ gave us in fulfilling God's purposes.

"The Word was made flesh, and dwelt among us" (John 1:14). "Because as he is, so are we in this world" (1 John 4:17).

YOU MAY WALK ALONE

When you know who you are and where you are going, there will be some people who will not be able to walk with you anymore. They know that they cannot manipulate you or cause you to compromise God's purpose for your life. They know their flattery and superficial compliments will not inflate your ego or cause you to lose focus of God's plan.

In fact, some people hang with you only because you inflate their egos. They don't care about you. They care about themselves. A typical scenario for a prisoner of prayer begins something like this:

"Hello, Sister Smith?"

"Yes, this is Sister Smith."

"Sister Smith, this is Sister Jones, and I need you to pray with me. My husband has threatened to divorce me, my son is on drugs, my dog bit me, my cat scratched me, and my roaches came out in the daytime! I need you to pray, because when you pray something happens."

Sister Smith replies, "Yes it does, doesn't it!" Sister Smith's ego is inflated because Sister Jones needs her. And she prays for Sister Jones each time Sister Jones asks.

But when Sister Jones begins to know who she is in Christ, when she finds she has a direct line to Christ through prayer, she doesn't need Sister Smith in the way she's needed her in the past. She can talk directly to God. She's not required to go through Sister Smith.

After a while, Sister Smith might even call Sister Jones to ask, "Is everything all right? You haven't called me to have me pray for you."

Sister Jones replies, "No, I haven't called you because now I know who I am in Christ and realized that I can pray for myself. In fact, I'm having a prayer meeting right now. Do you want me to pray for you?"

"No!" Sister Smith replies and hangs up. Sister Smith, instead of being happy that Sister Jones has found strength through her identity in Christ, is looking only to her own needs. She liked having Sister Jones depend on her. She liked the power that gave her.

Many single ladies hang out with each other so they can massage each others' wounds and hurts, talking about what some ex-husband or ex-boyfriend did to them. They find comfort in reliving the past and their role as victims. But when you start to know your identity, you can go on with your life and stop hanging around people who cannot let go of their past hurts.

Some who don't know their identity live their lives only through other people. Some wives live their lives through their husbands. Some husbands live through their wives. Even some parents see a second chance at life by living through their children. These are people who have no identity of their own. They are merely someone's wife, or husband, or parent. They have no purpose to motivate them. But when you begin to know who you are, you will develop your own sense of identity and purpose. You no longer have to live your life through other people. Your life will enhance others, not drain them.

When you know who you are based on Scriptural history, some people will be turned off by your confidence and assurance. They will not be able to intimidate you or make you feel that you need their endorsement in order to be somebody. You will not take an inferior posture or attitude to anybody. You will not give in to subservient mental attitudes that cause you to take on a spirit of failure, hopelessness, and defeat. Those who can't control or manipulate you anymore may even become fearful of you because of your boldness and will walk no more with you. They don't want you linked with God as it relates to who you are. Instead, they want to be your lord, or lord over you.

Many of Jesus' followers stopped walking with him. Many were offended by his claims and wouldn't believe him. Some were afraid because they saw the danger and potential violence associated with following him.

In the same way, when the Holy Spirit burdened me a few years back with the message of identity and the restoration of identity to blacks from a scriptural perspective, many of my constituents, both black and white, began to disassociate from me. They didn't disassociate because they didn't believe the truth but because they were concerned about their own reputations and desire to be accepted. Now that the message of identity has become popular and accepted by some well-known ministers, these same constituents are trying to reconnect. But I ask, are their hearts really pure and concerned about the truth and the will of God or just the honor and acceptance that comes from men?

Many blacks now are walking in the freedom of God's purpose and plan for restoration of ethnic identity. Many more will benefit in days to come. However, there are many whites who sit around and debate the issue of black identity and black history in Scripture. They should understand that the more they debate, the more powerful will be the declaration of ethnic identity from those held hostage to lies and misinformation for so long. Blacks who embrace these truths are becoming more fulfilled each day in their God-given destiny. They are being encouraged to walk out their purpose in life with more freedom and intent.

Are you offended? Will you walk away? Or will you join in this march of identity and purpose?

Chapter 8

Are You Offended?

Imust ask this question of many of my white brothers and sisters. Are you offended because blacks, as a people, are boldly proclaiming and confidently reclaiming their identity and heritage? Will you walk away from reconciliation and the purging of racism from the American church because you can't handle the truth about black identity from the Spirit of God? Are you offended by black equality? Remember, the principle is: first the natural, then the spiritual.

The Lord, by his Spirit, has chosen to bring forth corrective teaching regarding the rich heritage of black people in Scripture. This is an important step in reaching a people who have been stripped of their self-worth through organized racism and oppression. Are you offended?

This is an important question to ask and to answer. Are whites, especially white Christians and possibly some black Christians, offended because ethnic identity in Scripture seems to be the emphasis of the Holy Spirit in some parts of the body of Christ?

If you are, then ask yourself, *Why?* When the Lord desires to liberate a people so they can fulfill their God-ordained purpose, why should you be offended? This liberation necessitates a rooting out, a pulling down, a destroying, and throwing down of some of the misrepresentations of truth that have been taught. Why should anyone be offended?

But many are. As I travel across this country, I know that many whites are intimidated by the movement of the Holy Spirit in the black segment of the body of Christ. They don't understand what the Lord is doing or why he is restoring identity to black people through the truth of Scripture. And many are too prideful to inquire of black leaders what the Lord is doing in the black segment of the body of Christ. They usually voice their apprehensions and fears only to an "acceptable black," not to those leaders who are being used by the Lord in this particular thrust.

IDENTITY AND PURPOSE

Let me answer the questions they can't ask. Blacks must be freed from the chains of racism and from the myth of inferiority. We must be liberated in order to be able to take our rightful place in this world. To liberate a people, those people must have their history and identity restored, because that history and identity relate to God's purpose for that people. Blacks must know who they are from God's perspective, not from a society bent on defining us in such a way that keeps us inferior and under ungodly subjection. Others, too, must know who we are. What better source for accomplishing this restoration for us than the Bible?

Many whites criticize this movement by God. Some talk against it because they have not been given a leadership role in it. These are whites who still have the mentality that black people need to depend on them for leadership in everything, including ministry and fulfillment of God's plan. They are happy, cordial, and commending of ideas only when those ideas for a ministry to blacks are their ideas. And only when those ideas do not affect their comfort zones.

These whites get upset and label black leaders "racist" and the movement itself "harmful" to the unity of the body of Christ. What they really mean is it is "harmful" to their comfort zones. They get upset because black people do not need to depend on them anymore. A liberated black community hits many whites economically. They lose money when we grow as a people and become *producers*, not just *consumers*.

These whites need to recognize that the Lord wants to give purpose, identity, and destiny to our black leaders to strengthen our ethnic identity. They must understand that we as blacks need to know who we are and need to walk in that understanding. They need to stop the criticism and the claims of "racism."

Even some blacks do not welcome this change and would love for things to remain as they were. Odd as that may seem, it's true, for some blacks benefit economically and socially from the present state of blacks. There is an old gentlemen's agreement among some black leaders to "keep the people ignorant" so you can do what you want to do without accountability.

After more than twenty-two years of ministry and much searching of church history, I have never seen a move or thrust of the Holy Spirit that so affects black people, especially black men who, by the way, have been the greatest victims of organized and institutional racism. I have seen many black people rise up out of stagnation in life and take on brand-new challenges and new levels of obedience to God because they have been taught to know who they are. One of the most moving testimonies was from an inmate on death row. His mother is a missionary. He wrote to his mother, saying, "Mama, I may not get out of this. I've done the crime, now I must face the consequences. If I have to face death, I can now do it in dignity. After I read the book *Chosen, Not Cursed,* by Jefferson Edwards, I began to know who I am. Now I can face death."

He went on to say, "Mama, if I had known who I really am earlier in life, I would have never stooped so low or belittled myself to that level to have done those crimes."

After hearing this testimony, I cried, knowing the truth of Scriptural identity was affecting even black men who had lost all other support. Everyone had given up on them. Everyone but God.

RENEWAL, NOT RACISM

I think back to another movement, or "renewal," of faith, the Charismatic Renewal that began in the 1960s in white churches, among middle-class whites, mainly Catholics. There were no cries of racism from blacks back then, even though it was a movement primarily among whites.

I drove out from the inner city of Kansas City, Missouri, to suburban areas to attend the Charismatic conventions. Sometimes I was the only one darker than blue at those meetings. I received the Word of God, I read their books, bought and listened to their tapes, supported their ministries, and prayed for their leaders because I hungered and thirsted for God and the truth of God's Word. I didn't care what color the plate was that served me my spiritual food. I learned how to get the meat and leave the bones on the plate.

We did not cry racism when the only faces we saw on television in the Christian world were white faces. We supported their ministries, sent substantial offerings, called their prayer lines, and attended their money-making seminars. In fact, approximately forty-two percent of the financial support for national ministries came from black people. But we didn't cry racism.

We didn't cry racism when we looked at the leading Christian magazines and saw only white faces on the covers, white authors writing articles, white speakers for conventions and conferences. We bought magazine subscriptions and continued to support their ministries, but we didn't cry racism.

We didn't cry racism when the only books that we read in the Christian arena were written by white authors who taught from a white, middle-class perspective. We didn't cry racism when the only modern-day heroes of the Christian world that warranted an autobiography from publishers were white.

We didn't cry racism when Pentecostal and mainline Christian organizations formed associations but didn't invite black denominations, even those of the same influence, to come to meetings. We didn't cry racism when all the Sunday school quarterlies, textbooks, and Bibles showed only white biblical characters and even a white-

skinned, blond, blue-eyed Jesus. Although we knew this w:
mis-education, we had to use the only material available in
order to reach our people for the Lord. We used the material. We didn't cry racism.

Now the Lord is moving to restore black people's identity. He is using the truth of Scripture, bringing us back to
the reality that we are created in the image and likeness of
God. We are advancing in our relationship and union with
Christ. God is hearing the cry of black people who are praying what King David prayed, "Redeem me from the oppression of man, that I may keep your precepts" (Psalm 119:134).

We've only had a few years of teaching in the area of ethnic identity in Scripture, and nowhere is there the label that
some whites use now—black supremacy. We're "supreme"
now? Stop in the name of love! Maybe black identity, maybe
black awareness, and maybe black history in Scripture, but
not black supremacy. We are just trying to get on par.

There can never be unity or reconciliation between
blacks and whites until we see each other as *equal*. This
equality is found in the image of God and in the full redemption of Christ. We are all created in God's image. We are all
redeemed by Christ. Our country of origin is not a factor.
The color of our skin is just that, the color of our skin.

REMOVING THE OBSTACLES

The emphasis of restoring identity is for the *whole* body of
Christ. Lies that have divided the church must be elimi-
nated. Remember Jeremiah 1:10: "See, I have this day set
thee over the nations and over the kingdoms, to root out,
and to pull down, and to destroy, and to throw down, to

lant." This is part of the commission that God ation to racism in Christianity and in society. f rooting out, pulling down, destroying, and throwing down is a process that is hard for many to accept when you're working toward reconciliation between blacks and whites. Reconciliation in Scripture is restoring harmony by removing the obstacles. But first you need to identify the obstacles. And no one wants to identify the obstacles!

Oh, people want to have a little fellowship service or a foot-washing service once every ten to eighty years, do a little kissy-pooh and say everything is all right. Many do this in the name of reconciliation just to clear their conscience for a while, but they go back to the same practices of racism when they're out of that setting.

I see my task as identifying the obstacles between blacks and whites. Once known, those obstacles must be rooted out, pulled down, destroyed, and thrown down. Only then can we start building and planting a new race of people called "the church."

We can't build or plant anything good on the wrong foundation. A man cannot rise above his thoughts. A people cannot rise above their level of thinking as a people. That's why we must first remove the ungodly foundations and philosophies and ways of thinking. The first rule of the kingdom is to repent—to change your mind.

AN OBSTACLE

Let's look at one of the obstacles that keeps us from changing our minds and, as a result, keeps us from true reconciliation. Whites have been taught that they are *superior*. In fact, most of American society, including religion, is based on white superiority or supremacy. This is a lie that must be eradicated!

Blacks have been taught that they are *inferior*, led to believe that we were created for the bottom of society. Hypocritically, we are admonished to strive for the top, but what they mean is "strive for the top of the bottom." Whenever a few of us get off the bottom, that messes up this system. That is one of the greatest problems of a society based on a class system—somebody has to be on the bottom. In the American society, someone ordained that we're it!

God never ordained that blacks be on the bottom. But this present system did. This is a lie that must be eradicated!

These lies are produced by Satan, the father of lies (John 8:44) and embraced by the ideologies of men to bring division and strife among people and serve as a tool of oppression.

The truth is that God created all humanity in his image—no race superior or inferior. Many whites are offended and hurt by this declaration of truth. Many are offended by the true role of black people in the revelation of God to man throughout history that is substantiated in Scripture.

Yet the current movement to restore the identity and purpose of blacks based on Scriptural history will actually liberate white people as much as it is designed to liberate black people. The stronger the individual, the more benefit there is to all. When we work through a problem, we come out on the other side with a solution that works for everyone.

We as black people need to understand the black presence in Scripture, for only then are we able to walk in these truths. As these historical biblical truths become known in the black community, black people everywhere will rise up from their sense of inferiority and rise above the power structures that have held us down for so long. We as blacks can then take our rightful place in the leadership of the church— as apostles, prophets, evangelists, pastors, and teachers, bringing together the revelation of God's will for all people.

The attitude of the Christian community should be excitement and praise to God. But as we begin these changes, some white Christians are not at all excited. They are offended and intimidated.

There is no reason to be intimidated by what the Lord is doing in the black segment of the body of Christ. God is trying to liberate a people who have been shackled and imprisoned by oppression, racism, and inferiority for too long! God is sovereign. He can do whatever he wants to do, however he wants to do it, without asking for our permission. He is definitely not bound to the American way of life and its racist, oppressive practices and attitudes.

He has chosen, for this season, to liberate black people through the restoration of identity that is found in his image and his Son's redemption, and through the revelation of the Scriptures.

Don't find yourself working against the truth, because it is frivolous, for you can do nothing against the truth. Paul understood the response of people who were affected by his proclamation of truth. He understood that he had disturbed some of the comfort zones of the Jews of his day. With a sense of hurt, surprise, and disappointment, he asked the Jews, and I ask Christians today: "Am I therefore become your enemy, because I tell you the *truth?*" (Galatians 4:16, emphasis added).

Chapter 9

Christ Renews Man's Identity

Although man distorts man's identity through irrational religious philosophies and impractical, false teachings, the apostle Paul gives us a clear picture of what God thinks of us.

The church today also has an identity problem. Even the church of Jesus Christ does not know who she is and, as a result, settles for a place less than where God placed his church and his people.

Let us explore the question of identity, or who we are in Christ. Allow me to use the Bible, the greatest text ever written, to illustrate the point of renewed identity, purpose, and destiny. In the book of Ephesians, chapter one, the great apostle Paul was trying to tell us who we are. He did this throughout most of his writings.

Paul's pen drips with the confidence of his and our identity in Christ: "Blessed be the God and Father of our Lord Jesus Christ, who hath blessed us with all spiritual blessings in heavenly places in Christ" (Ephesians 1:3). Notice how Paul says "has blessed us." Paul was trying to get across that what God has done in Christ is a done deal! It's not something that is to happen in the future; it has already happened. In fact, before the foundation of the world, God had already made us somebody in Christ. Paul is trying to get us to see what God had already done and who we are in Christ.

Paul continues by saying, "... hath blessed us with all spiritual blessings in heavenly places in Christ" (Ephesians 1:3). The word "blessing" means to speak well of, fine speaking, commendation, reverent adoration. We get the English word *eulogy* from this word. Paul was admonishing believers to live in Christ and to let Christ live in us in order for us to reach our highest realm in life. We don't have to join a fraternity or sorority, a country club or social club, the toasters or charity organizations in order for the preacher to say good things about us when we die. The highest thing that can ever be said about us in this life has already been said about us in Christ. Thus it behooves us to abide in Christ. Christ has already given our eulogy.

"According as he hath chosen us in him before the foundation of the world" (Ephesians 1:4). Notice Paul says God *has chosen us in Christ.* His choice of us is a done deal! His choice of us has already happened, and Paul is trying to get us to recognize who we are and what God has done for us in Christ. "Wherein he has made us accepted in the beloved." Paul emphasizes that we are accepted and acceptable to God because we are in Christ.

If you are blood-bought and blood-washed, then you are accepted and acceptable to God. At Jesus' baptism, a voice came from heaven and said: "This is my beloved Son, in whom I am well pleased." If God is satisfied with his

Son, and I am in the Son, then God is satisfied with me. He's also satisfied with the way I was made in the natural, because he said it was good! Our noses may be different from other ethnic groups, but he's satisfied! Our hair may be different from other ethnic groups, but he's satisfied! Our talk and walk may be different, but he's satisfied! We may be hated in *this* society because of the color of our skin, but God is satisfied! Don't let anybody tell you that you are uncivilized, no good, dumb, lazy, and ugly. From the natural perspective, we're created in his image and likeness. From the spiritual perspective, if God is satisfied with Christ, and if you are in Christ, then he's satisfied with you. To the praise of his glory!

Paul admonishes us to remember who we are in Christ. He uses the past tense to help us realize what God had already done *before* the foundation of the world. Paul, through the Holy Spirit, is trying to get us to understand that our image, identity, and purpose originate in God and are restored, reclaimed, and renewed in Christ. It's up to us to appropriate these truths and live in freedom in Christ. For he told us clearly who he was.

Remember, if any man is in Christ, he is a new creation. God's original intent in creation starts all over again in Christ. That's natural *and* spiritual.

Chapter 10

One's Identity Is Linked to One's Purpose

We as black people do not know our identity. The church does not know its identity. Lost along with identity is our purpose.

But let me take you one step further. Ecclesiastes 3:1 states: "To every thing there is a season, and a time to every purpose under the heaven." Associated with purpose is timing. God "hath made of one blood all nations of men for to dwell on all the face of the earth, and hath determined the times before appointed, and the bounds of their habitation" (Acts 17:26). In other words, God had determined ahead of time where we would live and the appointed time and purpose in our being in these different places. The time element is important to the purpose.

God in his wisdom hides certain things until the appointed time. "It is the glory of God to conceal a thing: but the honour of kings is to search out a matter" (Proverbs 25:2).

Only a few people knew that Jesus was the Christ when he was born—Simeon, the old man awaiting the consolation of Israel, and Anna, the prophetess. The Wise Men from the East, who were black, also knew. They actually paid their visit to Jesus at his home when he was two years old. This was their appointed time. They arrived with a higher revelation of who Christ was than even the Jews had. They came seeking "[him] that is born King of the Jews" (Matthew 2:2). If many had known when Jesus was born that he was the Christ, he most likely would have been killed before he fulfilled his purpose. When King Herod found out about Jesus, he ordered the death of all male children two years old and younger.

It is important that we understand—and that the church understands—that the time has come for black people around the world. All those who have been victims of oppression and exploitation have not been able to understand their purpose in the Lord. They have been forced to be something they are not in order to survive and to satisfy the demands of those who enslaved them.

King David prayed this prayer: "Redeem me from the oppression of man, that I may keep Your precepts" (Psalm 119:134 NKJV). David, in this prayer, implies that as long as I am under the oppression of men, it will be hard for me to obey the Lord's precepts. Even if the importance of the purpose is made known to me, more than likely, as a black person, I will never fulfill it because of the oppressive systems of men.

This is why the Holy Spirit's present thrust to an oppressed segment of our society is to emphasize the need for identity based on Scripture; this is one of the first processes in the liberation of a people. Those who have participated in oppressing a people or have benefited may not appreciate such a thrust of the Holy Spirit because it indicts both the oppressors and those benefiting from oppression. It also makes people who have unknowingly added to the oppression of a people aware of their behavior. Since denial has been a way of life, this present thrust may cause controversy!

But I say "fear not" to our white brothers and sisters and to others who may not be benefiting directly or initially from this thrust. This movement by God is initially benefiting blacks, but others will benefit soon, because living in an oppressive system is also bondage. Those who participate in oppressing people or enslaving them economically are being used by Satan and don't even know it. That is why I say that this is a move of God based on Covenant, that God is delivering us from systems of men that have distorted and diluted true Christianity. As this visitation is received and understood, it will eventually affect the entire body of Christ.

I also say "fear not" to those who see this movement as rebellion. This is not rebelling against whites. It is rebelling against systems that not only have hindered black people as a race, but have hindered whites as well.

It's rebelling against systems that are fostering the racism in the church today. Look around you on Sunday mornings between the hours of nine and noon. These are the most segregated hours in the United States. Blacks go to their churches, whites to theirs, and Hispanics to their own churches.

This is why we Christians as a church lack power. The church, or should I say "our religion," has bought into the "system." We don't serve the kingdom of God; we serve the system.

That is why the Jeremiah 1:10 ministry must come first. There must be a rooting out, a tearing down, a pulling down, and a throwing down in order to be able to build and to plant the Word of God. That is why this current movement in the black community is not a rebelling against a particular people. It is rebelling against—rejecting—a system that is ungodly.

I believe every ethnic group ought to be able to find a sense of identity as that identity relates to Scripture. It is not racist to want to know your roots, your ancestors, your heritage. It is not racist to want to celebrate your heritage, to block off the streets, to have a parade. Every culture in America keeps its culture. Hispanics do it. Greeks do it. The Polish celebrate. But when blacks start to know who they are and celebrate their history and heritage, wearing the clothing from that heritage, people get upset. We're stepping out of line. Breaking the rules. We're antiwhite.

I say, those who are trying to keep us from our heritage are anti-us. Antiblack. We are finding out from God that we have been a part of God's revelation to man and a part of his purpose from the beginning. We are a part of his plan and of his revelation to man.

This uncovering of truth brings with it a sense of worth. It gives a sense of direction, a purpose to life. It allows us to stop trying to achieve the standards of an ungodly system and instead start to give ourselves to God for the rest of our lives as an instrument of righteousness. It is positive. It is strong.

If folks could only see what is happening, especially to black men who still are victims of oppression, they would recognize that this is a revival, a true visitation. They would see that blacks as an ethnic group are just one of those "nations" that the Gospel must get to, one of those ethnic groups whose time has come.

Chapter 11

The Message of Liberation

Liberation is a major theme of Old Testament history. In fact, the highlight of God's revelation under the Old Covenant was to deliver humanity from the oppression of sin, the devil, and oppressive and ungodly systems and nations. The liberation of God's people from oppressive systems was one of the reasons that God anointed Moses, the judges, and the prophets.

After the fall in the Garden of Eden, the Lord gave laws and ordinances to show humanity how to come back to God. He anointed Moses to oversee and administer the laws to his people. After Moses came Joshua, who led God's people into battle to take the land that had been promised to them by God. Before Joshua died, he addressed the people of Israel and encouraged them to obey the Law of God:

> Be ye therefore very courageous to keep and to do all
> that is written in the book of the law of Moses, that
> ye turn not aside therefrom to the right hand or to

the left; That ye come not among these nations, these
that remain among you; neither make mention of the
name of their gods, nor cause to swear by them,
neither serve them, nor bow yourselves unto them:
But cleave unto the LORD your God, as ye have done
unto this day. (Joshua 23:6–8)

Not only did the Lord encourage the people of Israel
to obey his Word, but he also warned the people of the
consequences of disobedience to his Word:

When ye have transgressed the covenant of the LORD
your God, which he commanded you, and have gone
and served other gods, and bowed yourselves to them;
then shall the anger of the LORD be kindled against
you, and ye shall perish quickly from off the good
land which he hath given unto you. (Joshua 23:16)

During Joshua's life and after his death, the people
remained faithful to the Word of God for a while: "And
Israel served the LORD all the days of Joshua, and all the
days of the elders that overlived Joshua, and which had
known all the works of the LORD, that he had done for
Israel" (Joshua 24:31; see also Judges 2:7).

But after the elders who walked with Joshua died, Israel
began to do what was evil in the sight of the Lord and
turned away from God's laws to serve other gods (see
Judges 2:11–13). The Lord's anger burned against the
people, and he gave them into the hands of robbers who
plundered them and sold them into the hands of their enemies around them, so that they could no longer stand
before their enemies (see Judges 2:14).

Wherever the people of Israel went, the hand of the Lord was against them for evil, as the Lord had spoken and as the Lord had sworn to them, so that they were severely distressed (see Judges 2:15).

But then the Lord raised up a judge who delivered them from the hands of their oppressors, or those who had plundered them (see Judges 2:16). But God's people chose instead to serve other gods from other nations. They eventually came under those gods and were oppressed or enslaved by those nations. Even though the people made this choice, it hurt God that his people forsook him. He became angry with his people, but he could not stay angry with them because he loved them even though they had turned their backs on him. Each time God's people disobeyed his command, he allowed them to be held in bondage or be oppressed by another nation.

Then, because God loved his people so much, he could not let his anger burn against them forever. Therefore, he raised up another deliverer/judge to liberate his people. This cycle of disobedience and deliverance went on and on. But God's plan was still being carried out. He had given these judges specific responsibilities.

These anointed servants were first used in ministry to help deliver God's people from the bondage of oppressive systems, judge them in their deliverance and freedom, and to ensure that the mind-set of having been oppressed did not continue.

The last part of the judges' responsibility was just as important as the first part. The Lord knew that when a people are under an oppressive system for a long time, they usually take on the attributes and values of the oppressor and that oppressive system. A people's culture, values, morals, and positive behavior patterns are usually swallowed up by the oppressive system. In fact, the oppressor, in order to manipulate and control, must make sure that any knowledge of and allegiance to the original heritage is suppressed or completely forgotten. The children of Israel, in forsaking the God of their fathers, lost their morals and were lured into different value systems, void of the ways of the Lord. The gods of the other nations had become sources for God's people. Because the true God was not the source of their living anymore, their lifestyles reflected bondage, ungodliness, and total compromise.

Bondage and compromise can become a way of life when you are not exposed to true freedom. Jesus said in John 8:38: "I speak that which I have seen with my Father: and ye do that which ye have seen with your father." In other words, you do what you see your fathers do. The word *father* means *source*. You do what you see your source do. If the gods of the other nations had become a source for God's people, then much of their way of life would reflect that source. Bondage can become "normal" when you are not exposed to freedom. Under such oppressive systems, you can end up compromising what you know is right in order to survive under that system.

Therefore the deliverer-judges were *anointed* by the Spirit of God to deliver the people of God from oppressive systems, to ensure that their lives, physically and mentally, were based on godly principles. They were to show the people of Israel what true *freedom* is under the true God.

BLACK HERITAGE

The plight of black people in America is quite similar to the plight of the people of Israel. Black people in America once had a rich heritage and their fathers were very much a part of God's revelation to man on the earth. Because of that heritage and culture, they had strong values, strong morals, strong families, and strong communities. Under slavery, however, these values were destroyed, the family structure was torn apart, and communities dissolved. If white slave masters were going to control black men for their labor and use black women for sexual pleasures and to breed to get more slaves, they could not let us keep the value systems we had in our native land and through our relationship with God. Black people had to learn survival under the oppression of slavery and the atmosphere of being declared less than human beings. Many whites in America during this time had, in theory, Judeo-Christian values. In practice, these values were not relevant when it came to treating black people with respect, dignity, and as people created in the image and likeness of God. What hypocrisy! Nevertheless, this is the way things were in America and, in some ways, still are.

We can see from the Old Testament that God was repeatedly liberating his people from oppression and ungodly systems and causing anointed deliverer-judges to help in this process. It is not a strange or new thing. It is the highlight of God's revelation to man under the Old Covenant. Liberation of God's people from ungodly and oppressive systems was one of the main reasons that God anointed the deliverer-judges and the prophets.

Under the New Covenant, Jesus started off with the theme of liberation. He dealt with the poor and the oppressed. "God anointed Jesus of Nazareth with the Holy Ghost and with power; who went about doing good, and healing all that were oppressed of the devil; for God was with him" (Acts 10:38). Anointing, simply stated, is the Holy Spirit's enabling power and ability.

Jesus' first proclamation after having been filled with the Holy Ghost was to deal with the oppressed. After he was tempted by the devil for forty days, the Scriptures say that he returned from the wilderness in the *power* of the Spirit: "And Jesus returned in the power of the Spirit into Galilee: and there went out a fame of him through all the region round about" (Luke 4:14).

After Jesus was tested in his flesh by the devil, the Bible says, he came forth in the *power* of the Spirit. The word *power* (*dunamis*) means force—special miraculous power (usually by implication, a miracle itself). English words that are derived from this transliteration are: ability, mighty, mightily, mighty deed, worker of miracles, power, and strength. One of the meanings of *power* is force or *violence*. In the Bible, God commanded his people to go into unholy, idol-worshiping nations and cities and utterly destroy everybody and everything—men, women, children, cattle, horses, houses, and temples. God's people accomplished these tasks by the power of the Spirit of God and by the command of his Word. Samson, a deliverer-judge for Israel, under the power of the Holy Spirit killed a thousand Philistines with the jawbone of an ass. If it had not been for the power of the Holy Spirit, Samson would have collapsed from sheer exhaustion. The Scriptures said that the Spirit

of the Lord came upon him and gave Samso
and the enablement to do this kind of miracul

A HOLY VIOLENCE

But under what dimension of the anointing was Samson operating? He was operating under a holy violence that came by the anointing of the Holy Spirit. Manifestations of this dimension of the anointing are seen throughout the Old Testament, especially when God is seen as a "Man of War," or the "Lord of Hosts," (the Lord Strong in Battle). There are many other examples in the Old Testament of how the Lord dealt with oppressive forces and power structures through the holy violence of the anointing, or the power of the Holy Spirit.

Even Jesus exhibited this holy violence under the anointing of the Holy Spirit when he overturned the money changers' table in the temple and whipped them with a scourge of cords. It was imperative that Jesus go in with a holy violence under the anointing, because that was the only way for God to get the money changers' attention. It is imperative that we deal with racism and violence with a holy anger and violence so we can get the attention of the church and the attention of the nation.

This anointing was needed in the Old Testament in order to deal with the oppressors who had enslaved God's people. It was needed in the New Testament to undo the works of the devil and overturn the effects of religion.

Jesus declared, after his forty days of temptation in the wilderness, that now, "The Spirit of the Lord is upon me, because he hath anointed me" (Luke 4:18). After the ıointing of the Spirit was upon him, Jesus immediately went toward "healing those who were oppressed of the devil." Everything that he was anointed to do dealt with liberating, delivering, and freeing the poor and oppressed. That was one of his major commissions.

But what happened to that commission? How did we lose the message of liberation that is so apparent throughout the Scriptures and in the life of Jesus himself?

Chapter 12

Somebody Dropped the Ball

King David prayed, "Redeem me from the oppression of men, that I may obey your precepts" (Psalm 119:134 NIV). This Scripture implies that as long as I am under the oppression of men, it will be hard for me to obey the Lord's precepts and purposes.

This really bothers me, because much of the world is affected by some system of oppression. That means that much of the world could possibly never fulfill their God-given purpose if these systems of oppression are not dismantled.

Yet the church, in large part, has not challenged oppressive systems, choosing to coexist with them and ignore one of Christ's major commissions—to liberate, deliver, and free the poor and the oppressed.

Somebody dropped the ball. Somebody left the court! Somebody left the game in relation to the message of liberation. This aspect of God's purpose has somehow been lost in modern theology.

The church of today is based on interpretation of the Bible. Remember that most of the commentaries and theology that shape the personality of today's church came from the British. Remember, too, that these writers and theologians were part of a culture that saw non-whites as inferior and that participated actively in the slave trade. Some were even die-hard advocates of slavery. In their writing they twisted the Scriptures and justified the concept of slavery.

The erroneous teaching of the "curse on Ham" was taught by many of these theologians. Some went so far as to say that black people were not human and did not come from Adam and did not possess a soul. This philosophy was passed on from Christian religion in Great Britain to Christian religion in the New World. That same philosophy was embraced by American government and even much of American society. This is why slavery was so accepted by the majority of the people when the United States was formed, and even sanctioned by the original Constitution.

With a theology that sanctioned slavery, the British theologians couldn't keep the liberation thrust that was a main theme in the Old Testament and is picked up again in the New Testament. They had to avoid that idea or indict themselves because the British were slave owners and purporters of racism and the oppression of people.

And so the mission of the church to deal with oppression and oppressive systems was lost. The British theologians gave us a gospel that basically supported the systems they were a part of and from which they benefited. The only emphasis on liberation was in relation to sin and the works of the devil. There was no message to support liberation of people from ungodly systems and nations even though we were commissioned to go into all the world and make disciples of nations. We were called to affect nations. But how can you affect nations if you don't affect the systems that control nations and set their policies? We basically received a "good-nigger" gospel that taught us to "accept things the way they are and don't expect anything to change."

In contrast, the true preaching of the Gospel of the kingdom of God is very militant and confrontational in nature. "And from the days of John the Baptist until now the kingdom of heaven suffereth violence, and the violent take it by force" (Matthew 11:12). This Scripture purports that the kingdom of heaven is surrounded by violent (forceful) men trying to keep us out of the Kingdom, but the violent (meaning those full of life) press into it with the same force of those trying to keep us out, and take it by force. This purports a militant, or aggressive, dimension of the church.

The Scripture also says that the kingdoms of the world will become the kingdoms of our God and his Christ (see Revelation 11:15). We are to make disciples of men and nations (see Matthew 28:19 NIV). We are to *compel* people to come. We are given power or authority over demons and unclean spirits and all manner of sickness and disease (see Matthew 10:7–8).

But somehow we lost this militant thrust of the kingdom of God. The British theologians gave us an interpretation and presentation of the Gospel that was conducive to their society. They benefited. They didn't give us a gospel that calls for things to change, especially in relation to slavery and oppression—and now racism.

Part 4

The Direction

Chapter 13

The Kingdom's Thrust
for This Season

On January 31, 1990, as I stood in the pulpit of the Reverend Turnel Nelson in Trinidad, off the coast of Venezuela in the West Indies, I made a declaration unrehearsed and unplanned. That declaration almost immediately began to come to pass. Speaking under the unction of the Holy Spirit and with the inspiration of God, I declared:

> This is a decade of freedom, and God's going to allow anyone who is crying out for freedom to experience freedom to whatever measure they can. But because many people don't know what real freedom is, they'll end up establishing more oppressive forms of government and control. Because of this time period, anyone involved in oppression in this decade of the '90s is coming down.

As I realized what I had said, I began to explain how this had already started in some nations. Haiti's oppressive reign of Duvalier had come down. The regime of Marcos in the Philippines had ended. Noriega was no longer in Panama.

I declared: "Concerning Communism, it's just a matter of time, it's coming down. Concerning the Soviet Union, it's just a matter of time, it's coming down. Concerning Cuba, it's just a matter of time, it's coming down. Concerning Nicaragua, . . . South Africa, . . . they're coming down." The crowd went wild in applause.

I also spoke that night of personal changes, in the home, in schools, in the church—of husbands oppressing wives, wives oppressing husbands, parents oppressing children, teachers oppressing students, pastors oppressing their flocks, bosses their employees, people their dogs. "If you are an oppressor, you are coming down!"

A few weeks passed, and Nelson Mandela was released from prison, starting the dismantling of apartheid in South Africa that finally saw Mandela become the country's first black president. In the next month or so, the Berlin Wall fell, and East and West Germany became one. The East European Communist bloc fell. The Communist strategy in Nicaragua failed. Even the Soviet Union fell.

Oppressive systems that we certainly expected would go on long after our lifetime, had crumbled. Quickly. I believe the Holy Spirit was working then to deal with the oppressors of this world, and is working today.

There's a fitting story in the Bible. The first visible expression of the kingdom of God is described in Daniel 2:32–45, where the prophet Daniel reveals and interprets King Nebuchadnezzar's dream. Daniel describes this great image that the king dreamed about:

> This image's head was of fine gold, his breast and his arms of silver, his belly and his thighs [sides] of brass, his legs of iron, his feet part of iron and part of clay.

Thou sawest till that a stone was cut out without hands, which smote the image upon his feet that were of iron and clay, and brake them to pieces. Then was the iron, the clay, the brass, the silver, and the gold, broken to pieces together, and became like the chaff of the summer threshingfloors; and the wind carried them away, that no place was found for them: and the stone that smote the image became a great mountain, and filled the whole earth.

This image is a picture of the systems of men. We call them kingdoms or empires or ruling powers. The "stone cut out without hands" is symbolic of Jesus Christ, the King of the kingdom of God. And the church, the instrument of his kingdom, smote the image. After the image became chaff, the "wind" (a move of God) carried the chaff away. Then, and only then, did the stone (the kingdom of God) become a great mountain that filled all the earth.

The essential thing that I want to point out, that I believe is missed by most people, is that the stone smote the *feet*, not the head. This is important because it puts a time factor on the direction the kingdom is moving in dealing with oppressive systems of men. Smiting the feet implies that the kingdom will, in the last days, deal with the foundation of the kingdoms of men.

Kingdoms of men promise freedom and prosperity, but end up forcing slavery and bondage on the majority, while those few in charge profit from their talents, their skills, and the labor of their hands and backs. These kingdoms of men, history has taught us, usually rob people of their resources instead of helping them to manage their resources.

God allows these kingdoms of men to exist. But based on the image of the stone smiting the feet, there comes a time when the thrust of the kingdom of God will be toward destroying or dismantling the foundations of these kingdoms of men. Then and only then will the kingdom of God (the stone) become a great mountain and fill all the earth.

Compare the same story as told in the New Testament, in Matthew 24:14, which ends: "And this gospel of the kingdom shall be preached in all the world for a witness unto all nations; and then shall the end come." God makes it clear that the Gospel cannot be preached in all the world until kingdom has risen against kingdom, nation against nation, until the earth is beset by famines and earthquakes. Not until the kingdoms of men have failed, or ceased to work, will people be interested in the good news of another kingdom—the kingdom of God.

I believe the Lord is allowing the kingdoms of men to exist until the church has matured enough and healed enough to deal with these systems of men. The church also must come to understand how much men have controlled and diluted the church with worldly standards of success while hindering it from being an instrument of God's kingdom.

I believe now is God's time to deal with oppression. The thrust of the mature church will be to dismantle systems of oppression that have affected people all over the world. I believe some segments of the church have already matured and understand the timing of the Lord to see the kingdoms of this world become the kingdom of our God and his Christ (see Revelation 11:15).

"To every thing there is a season, and a time to every purpose under the heaven" (Ecclesiastes 3:1).

Chapter 14

The Anointing and Freedom—
Old Testament and Today

> The Spirit of the LORD God is upon me; because
> the LORD hath anointed me to preach good tidings
> unto the meek; he hath sent me to bind up the bro-
> kenhearted, to proclaim liberty to the captives, and
> the opening of the prison to them that are bound;
> To proclaim the acceptable year of the Lord, and
> the day of vengeance of our God; to comfort all
> that mourn. (Isaiah 61:1–2)

These verses are very familiar to some and perhaps even a
favorite passage. But as this passage has been preached
and read over and over again, a very important truth has
been regularly overlooked or not emphasized. In this passage we see that the purpose of the anointing (the Holy
Spirit's enabling power and ability) is directly related to
freedom and liberty: "bind up the brokenhearted ... proclaim liberty to the captives ... opening prison ..." The fact
is, without the anointing there can be no freedom.

The passage also says that the anointing empowers children of God to "proclaim the acceptable year of the Lord. . . ." The summarized expression of the phrase can be explained through an Old Testament celebration—the Year of Jubilee. It takes the Holy Spirit's power to proclaim and respond to a year of jubilee, or a season of freedom, for a people.

THE YEAR OF JUBILEE

The Year of Jubilee was, for Israel, a year of emancipation and restoration. This celebration was kept every fifty years. The first principle was God's sovereign lordship over the whole earth, acknowledged by his people in their obedience to his command to set the year aside in this way. The Year of Jubilee proclaimed God as sovereign Lord of all: land, people, means of production, and life itself.

There were three commands that the Lord gave for each person in Israel to follow in a year of jubilee:

- "Return every man unto his possession" (Leviticus 25:10).
- "Return every man unto his family" (v. 10).
- "Ye shall not oppress one another" (vv. 14, 17).

When people are under oppression or an oppressive system, they will, more than likely, take on the behavior patterns of the oppressor. Since the behavior of the oppressor is all they see, it becomes easy to take that behavior as the model or standard. The Scripture implies that we do what we see our fathers (our source) do (see John 8:38). If people are not delivered from this mentality when they are freed, they will continue in the attitudes, behavior, and mannerisms of oppression and the oppressor.

This was clearly seen after our ancestors were freed from the chains of slavery. Many of them, even after they were emancipated, continued to have docile attitudes and dependence on the slave owner. They worked on the same land as sharecroppers, relying for their food and housing on the same ones who had held them slaves. Moreover, many envied the very ones who oppressed them. Proverbs 3:31 states: "Envy thou not the oppressor, and choose none of his ways."

This is a very sobering word for an oppressed people today. We have no business being jealous or envious of our oppressors when God has given us an identity, a purpose, and a destiny.

God is calling now for a season of freedom and restoration in the body of Christ. That puts him at odds with all that is contrary to that freedom. He therefore gives a space of grace to those who have been under oppression, to be delivered from its effects. During this time, whites must stop the behavior patterns of oppressing, and blacks must stop the behavior patterns of being oppressed. It will take the work and power of the Holy Spirit to teach whites not to oppress and to teach blacks a lifestyle of freedom and purpose. And with freedom comes responsibility. The Holy Spirit is waiting to anoint our lives and teach us how to live in freedom and be responsible for our own lives.

The anointing also is given in a season of jubilee to proclaim "the day of vengeance of our God." Along with a season of freedom (the acceptable year of the Lord) comes the proclamation that God is against and ready to deal with anything that is contrary to freedom. In this season, many people are surprised that the Lord is dealing with issues that seemingly he has winked at or even turned a blind eye to in times past. But now he will deal severely with anyone who continues in acts or attitudes that perpetuate racism and oppression.

Many in the church do not consider one of the purposes of the anointing as dismantling systems of oppression and evil power structures. They have not seen the obvious truth that we are to affect and change nations through the enabling power and ability of the Holy Spirit. We must be able to affect the spirit or systems that control nations in order to disciple nations (Matthew 28:16–20). Much of the world, approximately eighty to ninety percent, is under a spirit or systems of oppression, and because the truth of the anointing has not been fully realized, the church, in a large measure, has neither touched nor challenged these systems, but coexisted with them. We in the church present or interpret the Gospel in such a way as to go along with, instead of challenging, these systems in their ungodly practices of racism, discrimination, oppression of people, and bigotry.

The church does not have many preachers who are brave enough and yielded enough to the Holy Spirit to speak out against the oppressor and his practice of controlling people. In fact, much of the church world benefits from the way things are and has no desire for things to change. Religion that aids present power structures also rejects and is intimidated by the anointing of the Spirit to deal with oppression. Anyone who ministers at a high level of the anointing of the Spirit and the truth of God's Word will be labeled a "radical" and "militant." These labels are assigned because these preachers threaten present power structures of religion and society.

In dealing with oppression, controversy is inevitable. This is true because the oppressors have *power*, and they don't want to give up that power. They benefit from things remaining as they are. That way they stay in power. Anytime you bother a person's power, you are going to have controversy. In fact, people will kill you over the threat of losing power. Confronting oppression brought controversy and war in America—the Civil War.

GOD WANTS GENUINE RECONCILIATION

In July 1986, I attended a very important meeting in Dallas, Texas. Most of the leaders from the Charismatic and Pentecostal denominations were present. In that meeting, the Lord emphasized his desire, through men of God, for the churches in America to deal with the cancer of racism. If they did not, many of them would be excluded from national and international evangelism thrusts in the days to come. With eighty to ninety percent of the world's population made up of people of color, the message was clear that the Lord was not going to allow the American church to continue to export racism and bigotry through well-meaning white missionary ventures. The Lord also emphasized the need to begin a process of genuine reconciliation between black and white segments of the body of Christ in America. This thrust toward reconciliation was embraced by only a few of those leaders at that meeting.

Four years later, the real strong movement of the identity and freedom truths began to emerge in the black segment of the body of Christ. It was in 1990 that the Lord really began to deal with oppression and its effects and implications on the body of Christ and the world. Now is the season in which the Lord is making it known that he is dealing with racism in the church and providing freedom, through the anointing, to all those who are oppressed.

Truth is on our side. Remember, truth has the power to dismantle the present power structures and systems of oppression. This is the season in which the anointing of the Spirit and the preaching of the Word of truth will uproot everything and every person opposed to freedom and liberty.

Chapter 15

The Anointing and Jesus' Five Directives

And Jesus returned in the power of the Spirit into Galilee: ...The Spirit of the Lord is upon me, because he hath anointed me to preach the gospel to the poor; he hath sent me to heal the broken-hearted, to preach deliverance to the captives, and recovering of sight to the blind, to set at liberty them that are bruised, To preach the acceptable year of the Lord. (Luke 4:14, 18–19)

Just as liberation was a major theme in Old Testament history, it appears as a major theme in New Testament history as well. In fact, the passage above was taken directly from the Isaiah text quoted in the last chapter. Jesus' anointing to heal and liberate was prophesied, or predicted, years before he was born. The main thrust of the anointing on Jesus' life was directed at the *poor* and the *oppressed*. Jesus, under the new Covenant, started off with the theme of liberation and ministering to the poor and oppressed. In fact, part of the anointing on him was to give him enablement and the ability to deal with oppressive forces and power structures.

To "anoint" is to apply oil to a person or thing. The purpose of *sacred* anointing was to dedicate the person to God. The oil symbolized the Holy Spirit, empowering them for a particular work in the service of God. "The Lord's anointed" was a common term for a theocratic king. Jesus was anointed with the Holy Spirit at his baptism (John 1:32–33), publicly declaring him to be the Messiah (Luke 4:18, 21; Acts 9:22; 17:2–3; 18:5, 28). His disciples, through union with him, were anointed with the Holy Spirit as well (2 Corinthians 1:21; 1 John 2:20). Mark 6:13 and James 5:14 tell of Jesus' disciples anointing others with oil.

Jesus gave five directives in relation to the anointing that he received, which is an anointing we share in as well, especially those who are called to preach the good news of the kingdom of God. All five are related to freedom and liberation.

One of the main purposes of the anointing of the Holy Spirit is to take people from one state of being to an opposite state of being. The anointing takes a person out of a state of bondage and brokenness to a state of liberty and wholeness; out of captivity to a state of deliverance; out of blindness to an ability to see; out of poverty to a state of well-being; out of being bruised to health and freedom.

Let's look at each one of these directives.

PREACH THE GOSPEL TO THE POOR

The word *poor* in this passage means to be *bent over*. The poor are those who have been bent over due to being constantly placed on the bottom of a system. They are carrying the weight of others. They are not just physically but also mentally bent over. Being poor does not always mean the inability to work or produce; it also means to be under oppressive systems.

Blacks are considered the poor of this society not because we do not have the desire or ability to be at the top, but because we have been relegated to the bottom by class system ideologies and oppressive systems and individuals. God has not ordained blacks as a group, or any group for that matter, to be on the bottom, but our society has. Even if a black person has the educational achievements and necessary social qualifications, he or she is still viewed as one who *belongs* on the bottom of this society. If I am waiting for a ride in front of a hotel, wearing an official-looking dark suit, I could be mistaken for a bellboy and be asked to carry a white person's bags inside. The years on the calendar have changed in this society, but the mentality of many whites has not.

Black people are still viewed as doing only work befitting people on the bottom of the totem pole. Ignored by most whites are the advancements of black people in every facet of our society in spite of the many disadvantages they had to overcome in order to succeed. The ideology of blacks being on the bottom exists, and institutions and society in general are perpetuating this lie. Even our Constitution kept black people in a place of servitude and poverty. It stated that slaves (all black people) were only three-fifths of a human being. Religious theology of the day claimed that blacks did not possess a soul. Even though the Constitution was amended, the concept has remained in the hearts and minds of people. There is still a "three-fifths rule" in policies that deal with black people. I could graduate summa or magna cum laude from Harvard or Princeton University, but not be paid as much as a white person who graduated from Polka Dot University, in Polka Dot, Anystate.

Long after the Emancipation Proclamation of 1863, there were still organized efforts to keep black people in economic slavery. However, many former slaves progressed rapidly and moved up to a middle-class status. They were industrious, productive, creative, inventive, and unified. But whites blocked their way. A mere two years after the end of the Civil War, with former slaves making real progress, a white para-military organization called the Ku Klux Klan was formed in 1866 in Pulaski, Tennessee. Its intent was to hinder and stagnate these advancements.

There were lynchings, fear campaigns, and propaganda to keep the former slaves from moving into the mainstream of society. Most whites in the South did not accept the freedom of the former slaves. Even many whites in the North who agreed with freeing the slaves did not accept the amalgamation of the races. Even great preachers like Charles Finney, who preached the abolition of slavery, were against blacks and whites living or mixing with one another in society.

In 1883, the Supreme Court of the United States even declared the Civil Rights Bill of 1875 "unconstitutional." The Court said the Fourteenth Amendment merely forbade "states" from discriminating, not "individuals."

With the 1896 *Plessy v. Ferguson* case, the Supreme Court approved the principle of "separate but equal" treatment in transportation, paving the way for legal segregation ("Jim Crow" laws) across the country. The high court turned the enforcement of the "separate but equal" laws over to the individual states. In one generation, the segregation of the country had spread from transportation and education to hospitals, sports, even morgues and cemeteries. The signs went up: "Colored" and "Whites Only."

Then the states took away the vote from blacks by forcing them to pass literacy tests before being allowed to vote. Whites who couldn't read were still able to vote because of a "grandfather clause" that provided that if their ancestors had voted before a certain date, then they were entitled to vote. The date picked was always when blacks were not allowed to vote.

The Jim Crow Laws, along with the *Plessy v. Ferguson* case, literally kept blacks enslaved despite the Emancipation Proclamation and amendments to the Constitution. It was not until the case of *Brown v. the Topeka Board of Education* in 1954, that there began to be a little release from the slave master's whip.

Jesus came with an initial directive of preaching good news to the poor, that is, bringing good news to a poor situation. Psalm 119:105 says, "Thy word is a lamp unto my feet and a light unto my path."

When you preach good news to a person who is poor or in a poor situation, you are actually giving them a way out of their poor state and shedding light on their darkened path. The good news that Jesus preached to the poor was that he had come to set them free and that they did not have to remain in that state anymore. The best news that anyone can give to the poor is "you don't have to be 'po no mo.'"

HEAL THE BROKENHEARTED

The word *heal* in Luke 4:18 means to cure or to make whole. The word *brokenhearted* means crushed, shattered, or broken into pieces. One category of people that Jesus initially directed his ministry toward was those who were shattered or had been broken into pieces through oppression of the devil and through systems. Why would any society or people try to break or crush other people? Or why would even the devil break others? It is because they are threatened by the possibility of that person being whole and strong.

Again, that is the situation with racism and oppression in this country and abroad. This country, that once had a public policy of enslaving black people, now seems to be threatened by the descendants of those same people becoming whole and productive. There is an old fear among whites in our society that adds to the shattering or crushing of black people. That fear is that if blacks come to a state of wholeness, they are going to pay whites back for the way they treated blacks. Their rationale is that they did not enslave anyone. It was their ancestors who enslaved people, so why should they be responsible for what their ancestors did? This fear directly and indirectly perpetuates racism and oppression.

But there's another reason why many whites allow or even encourage racism. Many whites today still benefit from the way things are, and they won't do anything to change these ways that clearly are wrong.

From a black perspective, this fear that whites have about blacks coming to power or wholeness is ludicrous.

We are so glad to be free and whole, our first reaction is to party and celebrate and rejoice—not exact revenge on anyone or try to put anyone else down.

Jesus' directive, under the anointing, was to make whole or to cure those who were crushed and broken into pieces by the oppression of the devil, oppressive systems, and ungodly religious and political systems.

PREACH DELIVERANCE TO THE CAPTIVES

The word *deliverance* means freedom or pardon. Other English words that are synonymous with deliverance are *forgiveness* and *liberty*. The word *captive* means prisoner of war. This directive in Jesus' ministry was definitely related to freedom and liberation. These captives could be spiritual prisoners—of the devil, of sin, of ungodly habits. These captives could also be societal prisoners—of ungodly or oppressive systems and policies. It is clear that through the anointing, Jesus was to bring freedom to those who were captives. Jesus Christ's mission was to set the captives free! His mission was to bring the captives forgiveness and liberty and to not count their trespasses.

PREACH RECOVERING OF SIGHT
TO THE BLIND

The phrase "recovering of sight to the blind" means the restoration of sight. It implies to look up and to receive sight. It could mean the literal restoration of natural sight or it could mean the restoration of spiritual sight. The word *blind* means opaque (as if smoky). It also means to be without physical sight. It can mean to be without mental under-standing or perception. It also implies to be "enveloped with smoke" or "smoky." Figuratively, the word means to be inflated with self-conceit, high-minded, to be lifted up with pride, or to be proud. A further root word means to make a smoke or to be slowly consumed without flame.

This mission of the Lord in recovering of sight to the blind does not refer to just physical blindness but also blindness that comes by smoke that hinders you from see-ing and even damages your eyes.

One aspect of being poor or bent over is that you are always looking down. The anointing is to help people who were bent over to look up and receive sight. Their sight would be restored so that they could see God's plan and purpose for their lives. Their sight would be restored and the smoke would be cleared so they could see that they did not have to live under the control of the devil or oppressive men anymore.

Black people must be taught how to see again, because oppression and oppressors teach a person to see things in a way that reinforces oppression. Oppressors cover the truth with the smoke of self-serving lies and the haze of hatred, so that the oppressed cannot see clearly. Many of our race have been blinded by the smoke that comes from systems of oppression and even the smoke that comes through edu-cational and religious systems. Our people have been blinded spiritually, mentally, and physically. The philoso-phy of these systems has taught us over and over that we are inferior and meant to be on the bottom.

Some biblical interpreters have attempted to justify this treatment of black people through the erroneous teaching of the "curse of Ham." This curse, found in Genesis 9:18–29, is interpreted in this erroneous teaching to imply that black people, through Ham, were cursed and thus ordained to be slaves and to serve others. This teaching is ridiculous and reeks of a racist interpretation. The curse was placed on Canaan, not Ham. Moreover, this curse would have been fulfilled in a theological sense in Joshua 9:23, 27, where Joshua said to the Gibeonites, who are Canaanites,

> Now therefore ye are cursed, and there shall none of you be freed from being bondmen, and hewers of wood and drawers of water for the house of my God. . . . And Joshua made them that day hewers of wood and drawers of water for the congregation, and for the altar of the Lord, even unto this day, in the place which he should choose.

It didn't matter whether a curse was pronounced on Ham or on Canaan, because it wasn't God who pronounced the curse. It was Noah, who was drunk at the time. God doesn't honor what a drunk man says. God said in Genesis 9:1, "And God blessed Noah and his sons [Shem, Ham, Japheth], and said unto them, 'Be fruitful, and multiply, and replenish the earth.'" When God Almighty says you are blessed, you are blessed, and no one can overturn His blessing!

Ham is considered by most theologians to be the father of the black or dark-skinned race on this side of the flood. Ham's name means hot or dark, colored, or swarthy. He was considered to be the youngest son of Noah, the father of Canaan, and founder of many peoples (see Genesis 5:32; 6:10; 7:13; 9:18, 22; Psalm 78:51).

The Hebrew word for Ham means "hot" and is surely prophetic of the climates that have added to the blackness of skin of the Negro (the black), and the dark complexions of other peoples from the same stock. Egypt is called "the land of Ham" (Psalm 105:23), and the Egyptian word for "Ham" is Kem, meaning black and warm. From Ham we have the Egyptians and Ethiopians (Cushites), or what we now call Africans, Babylonians, Philistines, Mongolians (Chinese and most other Oriental people), and Canaanites. The darkest of the people of color came through Ham's son Cush. But other people of color came through his other sons, Mizraim, Put, and Canaan. The sons of Cush were Seba, Havilah, Sabtah, Raamah, Sabteca, and Nimrod. Grandsons, whose father was Raamah, were Sheba, and Dedan (see Genesis 10:6–20).

You must also realize that Noah's son Shem was a person of color and so was Japheth. I do, however, believe that the fair-skinned race did eventually evolve from the lineage of Japheth. Color was the norm, and that's why even today, approximately ninety percent of the people in the world are people of color. Only ten percent are considered fair-skinned or white.

Much of this erroneous teaching has been smoke to blind the eyes of people of color in order for them to take an inferior posture in relation to systems of oppression. One definition of "blind" was to make a smoke or slowly consume without flame. This is what has happened in much of the educational system of this country. Without using physical restraints and physical enslavement, the educational system in this country, and many other countries that have been ruled by colonialistic ideologies, have kept black people and other people of color in a subservient or inferior mental state.

This society, through its educational system, has blinded the minds of our people. In most schools in this country, the majority of the year is spent studying white heroes. World history, in most schools, begins with Alexander the Great. How can anyone study world history and ancient and modern civilizations without studying about Africa, where civilization began? When black students study about whites and their accomplishments and fail to get a healthy diet of blacks and their great accomplishments, they will see themselves as inferior to whites.

In 1832, there was an organized effort to establish an educational smoke screen to blind black people. Senator Henry Berry, from Virginia, in an address to the Virginia House of Delegates, stated:

> We have as far as possible closed every avenue by which the light may enter the black Slave's mind. If we could extinguish the capacity to see the light, our work would be complete. They would be then on the level with the beast of the field and we should be safe.

This statement by Senator Berry reveals a definite plot, through education or a lack thereof, to hinder light or sight to the minds of black people. This ongoing practice of an oppressive system is threatened when black people begin to *see* who they really are. Remember that the object is to bring light so we can see: "Thy word is a lamp to my feet and a light unto my path" (Psalm 119:105); "The entrance of your words giveth light" (Psalm 119:130).

One of the foundational missions of the Lord, through the anointing, was to give sight to the blind. He came to remove the smoke of systems that blind people and keep them from looking up and seeing. He has given us the same anointing to keep us from being slowly consumed.

One definition of "blind" is to inflate with self-conceit or to be high-minded, or to be lifted up with pride, or to be proud. The Lord also came to deal with people who have become high-minded or inflated with the air of superiority, believing that they are justified in oppressing people, controlling their lives, and keeping them bent over.

The Lord has come to deal with the oppressor. The Lord will clear away the smoke and the haze that have been blinding people so they see themselves as superior and practice a doctrine of white supremacy, feeling justified and compelled to oppress black people as a way of life.

TO SET AT LIBERTY THEM THAT ARE BRUISED

The word *bruised* means crushed. This is the same as brokenhearted. The Lord has come to liberate those who have been crushed, those who have been pushed down by oppressive systems and kept on the bottom.

When you crush someone, you take away his or her form. You take away his or her culture, heritage, history, morals, values, and every other essential thing that helps to make that person who he or she is. Remember that a person's morals and values are passed down with their culture. The way a person acts and behaves is based on the culture and heritage, that was passed down from previous generations.

In America today, and in many other parts of the world, there is a cry to return to values and morals. But in America, the things related to the values and morals of black people—our culture and heritage, along with godly influence and principles—were stripped away by a society that was threatened by us and by our connection to God.

In America, black people were crushed during slavery, broken again during Jim Crow days, and are continuing to be crushed today through more sophisticated, subtle systems of oppression and racism.

When you are crushed, you cease to be who you are. You lose your identity. Once you lose your identity, losing your purpose in God's creation is inevitable. During slavery, we were separated from our culture, history, values, and, most of all, our God.

Blacks were the only race that the American system put in the "melting pot" in order for us to lose our form and sense of heritage. We were the ones the system wanted to crush and change into a new form. You see, America is not a melting pot. It is a stew or a salad. In a stew, the potatoes don't lose their identity as potatoes. Nor do the carrots lose their identity as carrots, and the beef does not lose its identity as beef. The potatoes season the carrots. The carrots season the potatoes. And the carrots and potatoes season the beef. The ingredients of the stew are all seasoned by each other, while remaining what they are. When those same vegetables are crushed, they can no longer be identified. They become a mush. When you are crushed, you cease to be who you really are. You lose your purpose in creation, for the way you were made is related to your *purpose* in life.

Jesus came to set at liberty those who were crushed or ground to powder in their environment. He came to cause us to have form and not be void by allowing the Word of God to shape us into his purpose. God created us by saying,

"Let there be . . . ." He will add to what we are by continually saying, " Let there be . . . ." and we shall become what he wants us to be.

TO PREACH THE ACCEPTABLE YEAR
OF THE LORD

"LORD thou hast heard the desire of the humble: thou wilt prepare their heart, thou wilt cause thine ear to hear: To judge the fatherless and the oppressed, that the man of the earth may no more oppress" (Psalm 10:17–18).

The Word of God is very clear on the issue of the Lord dealing with oppressors: The Lord "shall break in pieces the oppressor" (Psalm 72:4). The Lord's eyes are upon all those who are oppressed and he promises to deliver: "He (the Lord) shall redeem their life from oppression and fraud and violence" (Psalm 72:14, AMPLIFIED).

The anointing during the ministry of our Lord was to help us to recover our sight, to clear away the haze and smoke, so that we could see who God is, who Jesus Christ is, and who we are.

The church in this "year of the Lord" can experience and enjoy a time of true emancipation from the slavery of racism and fully experience racial restoration. But to do so, whites and blacks must submit to the anointing of God through the power of the Holy Spirit. Both must acknowledge that God is the sovereign Lord over all people, and that all are created in his image and likeness.

There is no room for ethnic superiority and inferiority. There is only one Boss. There is only One who is superior—the *Sovereign Lord!* For believers, this means whites must submit to his leading, his guidance, his lordship. This means whites must allow the Spirit of God to be Lord over their racist traditions, prideful heart, oppressive attitudes, and prejudiced behavior against blacks. There is one Head in the church—Jesus Christ. The members of the body of Christ take direction from the great Head of the church, and the anointing of the Spirit flows from the Head to the rest of the body. The Holy Spirit gives each of us the power to carry out these directives from Jesus Christ.

Part 5

The Problems, the Rewards

Chapter 16

God Is Talking to Us Now— We Need to Listen

I study church history and try to see patterns that are based on Scripture. And I haven't found any move that has directly affected black men in the last hundred years—until now. In fact, not a whole lot has affected any of the black segment of the body of Christ in any large way. Except Azusa Street. That movement, the beginning of the Pentecostal Church, was started in 1906 in a mission on Azusa Street in Los Angeles. This revival did affect blacks and spread to churches across the country. Almost sixty years later, in the 1960s, the Charismatic movement had some effect, but it is dissipating.

In my twenty-two years of ministry, I have never seen God talk to us as straightforwardly as he is talking to us now. He is talking to us where we live.

Although the church is called the pillar of truth and the ground of truth, I have noticed how the church runs from truth and reality. Life in the body of Christ has become a place where people do not want to deal with the real world.

This is why we have so many people under the bondage of drugs, welfare, crime, and a class society. If we are going to purge racism from modern-day Christianity, we must deal with and confront the horrible realities of our society. We must not be afraid to tell the truth about these realities. We must preach the pure Gospel of the kingdom of God—especially to black people. And we must trust God to bless our efforts.

It is not a new thing to use the Gospel for personal means. It is no longer a surprise to anyone when you say that the Gospel of the kingdom of God was not preached to the people of African descent. We as black people received an adulterated gospel—a gospel mixed with the bitter herbs of racism, a gospel mixed with the poison of hatred, and a gospel that was mixed with the broth of white supremacy. This gospel kept us dependent on the white slave owners instead of encouraging us to be dependent on the all-wise God of heaven. This gospel that the white religious world preached to us kept us looking for heaven in the sky to keep our minds off the hell of slavery on earth.

It is time for an era of corrective truth. We are rooting up, pulling down, throwing down, and destroying lies that have oppressed our people for decades, and then we are going to build and plant truths that liberate and deliver. We must purge racism from modern-day Christianity through the unadulterated Gospel of the kingdom of God.

In an attempt to find an identity with those referred to as God's "chosen people," many European whites became Jews—by religion. They joined the Jewish religion. They didn't have to do that. They already had their own identity, made in the image and likeness of God.

During the Renaissance, many scholars and religious leaders distorted history by making Jesus and everything related to Christianity fit into a European mold. Christianity became very popular, and many Europeans embraced Christianity. They even depicted Jesus as looking like them, even though there are Egyptian artifacts depicting Jesus and Mary and people of that era as having more of the Hebrew or Negro features.

Remember that during the reign of the Roman Empire, the Romans had free access to the world as it was known. They controlled the highways, shipping, and armies of the world. Therefore, they carried the Gospel farther than any other people. But the Gospel they carried was interpreted from a perspective that benefited them. It is my opinion that they used the Gospel as a tool to oppress people. The Romans used religion to bind a man's spirit so that they could oppress that same man physically, psychologically, and financially. So they interpreted the Word of God deceitfully, for the benefit of themselves, not as God had intended it to be preached.

The Lord's Commission focuses on us taking a pure, unmixed Gospel to every nation. "And this gospel of the kingdom will be preached in the whole world as a witness to all the nations, and then the end will come" (Matthew 24:14 NKJV). "Go therefore and make disciples of all the nations, baptizing them in the name of the Father and of the Son and of the Holy Spirit, teaching them to observe all things that I have commanded you; and lo, I am with you always, even to the end of the age" (Matthew 28:19–20 NKJV).

God is genuinely concerned for *all nations*. The Greek word for nation is *ethnos* and means race, as in belonging to the same culture or of the same habit. Our English phrase *ethnic group* is derived from this term.

The Gospel of the kingdom is the rule of God, the reign of God, the throne of God, the government of God, and the dominion of God. This must be preached to all the world, right down to the country, the city, the household, the family, and to the individual—as a witness (an evidential lifestyle) to every nation (every race). Then the end shall come. The Gospel of God's reign and rule is meant to get to every race and ethnic group. The Gospel is to be purely preached to every nation, not out of superficial charity or racial supremacy, but because a gracious God is concerned for every race, every tongue, and every color.

A PERSONAL GOSPEL

To reach every race, every tongue, and every color, this preaching of the Gospel must become personalized. In fact, the entire New Testament is based on a personal relationship. We emphasize that each person should have a personal relationship with Jesus Christ. We have the assurance that he feels our deepest pain, hears our deepest sighs, and that he will personally deal with what affects us most. The Scripture even says that he is "touched with the feeling of our infirmities" (Hebrews 4:15).

But black people did not receive a personal Gospel. We have had a Gospel perpetuating the idea that you have to look a certain way or talk a certain way to be acceptable. The message was that "made in the image and likeness of God" meant "like white people." As if God's likeness was the same image as white people. As if black people were *not* made "in the image and likeness of God." But we were, and we are.

Jesus says, "Repent ye: for the kingdom of heaven is *at hand*" (Matthew 3:2, emphasis added). The kingdom is meant to deal with what is near or *at hand*. We as blacks haven't had much gospel that deals with what is at hand. We've heard, "It will get better by and by"; "Don't worry about it baby—joy comes in the morning, but weeping endures for a night"; "One day we'll fly away." Or we hear about the good old days, which doesn't look like it did much for those who brag about them, because they are just as ignorant now as they were years ago. Religion either enshrines the past or glorifies the future. What religion must do is deal with realistic things "now."

The Gospel of the kingdom must affect every race and nation. This implies that the Gospel must affect every spirit that is controlling that nation or race. The Gospel of the kingdom must affect every system, every bondage, every institution that is directly opposed to the will and way of God. The thrust of the Gospel of the kingdom is to tear down empires and systems that oppress people and lands. Black people did not get this teaching. Most of the personality of the church today was shaped by British theologians who gave us a passive gospel, a gospel that always waits for something to happen—one day.

Had they given us an active gospel, they would have indicted themselves. Had they given us a gospel that overturned and challenged evil and oppressive systems, they would have jeopardized their own power structures that were perpetuating and endorsing slavery and racism.

Knowing these distortions, we must now build the nations through the preaching of the true Gospel of the kingdom. We have the ingredient for building nations—righteousness. "Righteousness exalts a nation" (Proverbs 14:34 NIV). Righteousness comes by the revelation of the Gospel. In Romans 1:16–17, Paul says, "I am not ashamed of the gospel of Christ: for it is the power of God unto salvation, to every one that believeth; to the Jew first, and also to the Greek. For therein [in the Gospel] is the righteousness of God revealed."

A DIFFERENT STANDARD TODAY

Righteousness is not regimented; it is revealed. Righteousness means to be in right standing with God and with one another. There is a standard of righteousness that is different today than it was years ago, and that is why it must be revealed by the Spirit. We are facing the deterioration of families, cities, and nations. We are facing sin and unrighteousness in every facet of our society. We are caught in the grip of an epidemic of crack cocaine addiction. Teenage pregnancy with no thought of ever getting married is now normal. When young black men leave home, too many today are going to prison instead of to college. Almost half of our black children today are born into poverty, knowing only their mother, not their father, sometimes knowing neither. These children start life with little hope of doing any better than either parent.

The only way we can overturn unrighteousness is by bringing forth the righteousness of the kingdom. The only way we can illuminate the darkness is by shining the light

of the kingdom into all the dark places. T
nity needs a personal Jesus, not a gene
percent of the young black men in our co
never walked through the doors of a church.
take them a Jesus who is relevant to their lives. We ne
take them a Jesus who touches the lives of gang-bangers,
drug dealers, addicts, and those who abandon their children. We need to take a personal Jesus to the streets—a
Jesus who understands their wounded hearts, who feels the
intensity of their pain, but who also sees their unlimited
potential for the kingdom of God.

If we are going to purge racism from modern-day
Christianity, we must embrace and preach the Gospel of the
kingdom boldly, so the kingdom can reach every race, every
nation, every city, every neighborhood, every family, every
individual—to the praise of his Glory!

But the first and greatest battle we have is the battle
over our own selves. "He that is slow to anger is better than
the mighty; and he that ruleth his spirit than he that taketh
a city" (Proverbs 16:32). Then the Scripture says, "He that
hath no rule over his own spirit is like a city that is broken
down, and without walls" (Proverbs 25:28). When you're a
broken-down city without walls, anything can come in. You
are without a defense. We all are dealing with all kinds of
influences and powers and we must have influence over
ourselves.

People have been sent out to disciple nations who were
not really disciples. We produce seed after our own kind. *Disciple* means learned of, taught of, followers of the Lord. That's
why many of us are not going to be involved in true spiritual
warfare. Because we have no discipline. Many Christians are

nost undisciplined, lazy people in the world. They never
nt to Christian boot camp. We don't want anybody to tell
us anything; we don't want any regulations. And because of
it, we're not qualified for the Lord's army.

Those who choose to be involved in nation building
must first take dominion over themselves and learn discipline. The seed of the kingdom, which is the rule and reign
of God, must get in *your* earth. You can then take it to the
ends of the earth.

THE ENDANGERED SPECIES

We are also in a "war of ideas," and we haven't learned how
to fight it. In fact, we haven't even recognized it as an enemy.
Many historic churches used to have a kingdom-dominion
emphasis. They understood that the church was here to literally take over. That's been washed away in many denominations. This is a whole different load that God has put on
us. It affects everything I have said thus far in the church I
have pastored for twenty-two years. It affects everything I
have said in my traveling ministry for more than twenty
years. This "war of ideas" is rendering us powerless.

Even before the church was founded on the Day of Pentecost, the Israelites in the wilderness kept wanting to be like
other nations. Which means, the real war zone *is inside us.*
There is a battle going on between heaven and hell in our
soul and in our spirit. The soul is our intellect, reasoning,
emotions, will, mentality, seat of affections, our attitudes and
aptitudes. The enemy wars against what God says. "Hath
God said?" was the first question that Satan asked man.

Satan isn't interested in us until there is conviction
faith that comes by what God has said to us in the Word o
God. As the church, we are to be offensive, moving forward
against whatever doesn't match what God says.

Instead, we've become defensive against attacks to our
faith and conviction. We as a church have become apolo-
getic. The church no longer tries to annihilate ungodly and
sinister ideas. We compromise, coming to common ground
with other kingdoms. We rationalize, saying that there is
some truth in what others say. We coexist with other ideologies and render our own ineffective.

We're not supposed to compromise and coexist; we're
supposed to annihilate those ideas that are contrary to the
Word of God. We are to be offensive in presenting the
truth. We are to reach every man's conscience through the
manifestation of that truth. You never defend what you
believe; you speak it. You walk it. We never apologize for
what we believe. We just declare it, and if you can't believe
it, you're the one in trouble.

Proverbs 23:7 says, "For as he thinketh in his heart, so
is he: Eat and drink, saith he to thee; but his heart is not
with thee." As we think in our heart, that is really who we
are. God said that what is going on in our thoughts is really
us. In the religious world, we know how to put the face on.
We know how to act submitted, but we know inside we
have rejected everything that has been said.

As a man "thinketh in his heart, so is he." The truth is, a
man cannot rise higher than his thoughts! God can say
something, but if you think you can't do it, you won't. That's
why we have to learn to take control of our thoughts. If we

to harness our thoughts to agree with what

more truth: A people cannot rise higher
thinking as a people. This is where we
are as a people and this is one of our main dilemmas—the
way we think. Some people have told us how to think to
keep us at a certain level. And we keep going to those folks
to endorse us. When we do that, it doesn't matter what
doors open, what opportunities present themselves, how
much training we have. If we are thinking, "I'm poor, my
mama was poor, I can't do any responsible job," then we
won't do a good job and we won't succeed. We as a people
won't rise higher than the level of our thinking.

We are in a deadly war with ideas. Satan has been wag-
ing a war of ideas against the church and against people,
and if we lose this war, this time, we will surrender our children to Satan for at least the next two or three generations.
We can have them in church every Sunday, but if we lose
this war of ideas, we'll lose them.

Consider our young people of today. Sixty percent of
our black teenage girls will end up pregnant and almost 100
percent of these will remain unmarried. Half of our black
young men will be arrested before they are eighteen years
old. A large percentage of our young black men will be
killed or die before the age of twenty-five. Sixty-seven percent of the male prison population is made up of black
men, yet black men make up only six percent of the country's population. Prisons are being asked to do what parents
aren't doing—discipline our children.

Our families aren't two-parent families. Seventy percent of black families are headed by women. In large urban

areas, up to eighty percent of black families are headed by women. It's shocking to realize that there is no man in seventy to eighty percent of black families in the United States and women say: "I don't need no man."

We are raising a generation of young men who probably will end up in prison. One out of every four of our men ages twenty-one to thirty is in prison now. In just one year, the percentage of black men in prisons went up ten percent, from fifty to sixty percent, and now stands at sixty-seven percent. Most of that increase was *young* black men, a direct result of our men not being in the home.

There is no future for us as a people if these diabolical statistics are allowed to continue with no effort from us to stop them. We ought to take seriously the problems in our communities and in our homes. We ought to be frightened because today the black family and the black man are endangered species.

Chapter 17

Overturning Systems

When the kingdom of God is truly manifested in the world, oppressive systems will be overturned. Two of the systems that have affected black people that the kingdom of God must now overturn are the *class* and the *welfare* systems.

The first is *classism* or a *class society*. The people who control the class system have set up certain ways of thinking in society in an attempt to control our minds. One of the most effective tools that people who promote classism use is education. In education, a person is programmed to think that he or she cannot rise above their own level of thinking and that certain people were created to be on the bottom. They use grades and labels (remedial education) and test scores. And comparisons. Always comparisons that put people down.

So, in effect, education helps to keep class systems going. Among the men and women who shaped the educational systems of the world were those who were proponents of class systems. And their principles remain. We send our children to school and when they come out we wonder why they cannot pursue the things of God and why we cannot control them.

Education has always been a stronghold for any world power. I believe there are three basic foundations of a nation: education, government, and religion. It is through education that a nation molds and indoctrinates the minds of children. It is through education that a nation determines what a person should think, how a person should think, and when a person should think.

The educational system was actually the trigger for the civil rights movement that had its beginnings in the 1954 *Brown v. the Topeka, Kansas, Board of Education*. Blacks rebelled against a system of education that taught segregation and provided an inferior education that kept us in our "place" rather than helped us reach our full potential. Most of the riots in 1965 were by students who would not accept a glorified apartheid system anymore. I was one of those students.

Many young whites also rebelled, but their focus was the hypocritical system of their society. These rebelling whites were progressive and liberal. They marched with us to right the wrongs of the world. It's interesting to note that these same Hippies and Yippies were the first recipients of the Charismatic renewal in the church community in 1967 that began to challenge the traditions of the church.

But those days are gone. Today there is a war that goes on every week in our schools. In this war, the enemy is after our seed. Our children leave home to attend public schools where they are indoctrinated with all kinds of ideologies and philosophies that are opposed to the Word of God. They are teaching our children how to think. Black children in particular are casualties in this war. They are exposed to ideas that relegate them to an inferior posture. Until recently, the "heroes" were all white. By the time a student got to high school, the only required reading of "literature" was *To Kill a Mockingbird* and *Huckleberry Finn*. Both portray blacks as docile and shiftless. Unless teachers give black students more assignments with a different black focus, there isn't a lot that our students read in school that reinforces the self-worth of blacks.

Why do you think so many white teenagers are so full of superiority, hatred, and anger toward black people when the '60s saw black and white students working together? The reason, I believe, is because they have gone through the "best" educational system of our society. They have gone through a system that reinforces ideas that they are superior and blacks are inferior. Sometimes these views are blatant but most of the time they are very subtle. A student may not realize the attitude gained from a particular lesson. But the "lesson" is there, and it's very effective.

There is a new escalation of hate coming. We are growing a generation that is intolerant of others. Some of the same white people with whom I was socially involved back when we were students, people I listened to music with, now have children who would shoot me if they had the chance. They're not learning from history.

I want these students to know black history, to know that our people were forced from their native land in chains, that thousands of black people died at sea, never making it across the Atlantic Ocean to the Americas or the Caribbean Islands. I want them to know what life was like for black slaves in the colonies and then in the states. I want them to see the beatings, the deaths from beatings, the mothers being torn from their children to stand on an auction block to be sold to another owner, never to see their children again. And I want them to know about those who ran away and made it to freedom and a decent life, and about those who ran but were caught and whipped. I want them to know the horrors of slavery. I want them to know about the fear that blacks have lived under since slavery, the lynchings, the torching of homes. I want them to know the truth. I want them to care, so these evils will never happen again.

THE USE OF FEAR

The educational system needs to look at why it is so easy for white supremacist groups, with racism as their main agenda, to recruit young whites for the Skinheads, White Patriots, Church of the Creator, and the Knights of one state or another. They use fear, the same fear that worked so well years ago on poor whites by racists claiming that blacks, unless they were kept in their place, would take their jobs and their chance for a decent house. White students today are told that their generation will be the first that does not do better economically than their parents did. The blame is still on blacks, but now the claim is that affirmative action laws are hurting whites in the job market. It's a tactic of fear, it's racist, and it works. It breeds hate.

It is my contention that it does not matter how much progress a black person makes in this country. If this country keeps the same archaic and oppressive educational system, it will turn a person back to class philosophies. We have changed economically, politically, socially, but we have not changed educationally. Therefore, some children of whites are full of hatred and anger toward black people because the educational system in our society continues to propagate the ideas of racism and classicism instead of preparing every student to compete fairly in the job market.

Likewise, after all the struggles, boycotts, and beatings during the civil rights movement, many black youth have gone back to a docile, do-nothing way of life. Many of our young people have nothing to do, and they don't want to do anything. Many won't even try. Some are hanging on corners and holding up walls as a profession. Why is it that many of our young people have no motivation to work, to achieve, and to realize their potential? Because the educational system was not changed. Its ideologies and philosophies have poisoned an entire generation. The educational system did not have their best interests at heart. It doesn't help us advance. It doesn't promote self-worth, self-actualization, or any motivation to achieve. It is void of any righteous foundation from God to help impart right morals and values.

That's why the church must begin training our children. God never gave the world permission or the responsibility to train our children. It is the responsibility of the parents and the church to train our children. But we have allowed them to drink the milk of knowledge from Greek philosophers and men and women who are proponents of oppression and classism. We should not be surprised when hatred, anger, and inferiority are manifested in their lives.

We must set up a bulwark to stop the ungodly philosophies and ideologies that have promoted a view that sees black people as second-class citizens who belong on the bottom of the ladder. The education that blacks received was poisoned by colonialism. It was poisoned by racial discrimination, governmental manipulation, humanism, and Western philosophy. How are we going to raise a generation for the Lord if we are sacrificing our children on the fiery altars of the Molechs and Baals of this present educational system? It is my opinion that we cannot raise a generation for the Lord if we keep our children under the present public educational system.

You would be interested to know that by the time our children are eighteen years old, they have had 38,000 hours of Western philosophy. If those same children had gone to every Sunday morning service, Sunday evening service, and Wednesday evening service in those years, each would have had only 4,000 hours of Christian education. It does not take a rocket scientist to figure out that we are raising a generation indoctrinated with lies instead of truths of life, with information that stifles their progress and clouds the purpose for their lives instead of motivating them to realize God's amazing destiny for their lives.

DE-WESTERNIZING EDUCATION

It is imperative that we as blacks develop our own educational system, with our own books, our own history, with a goal that brings God glory. I believe God is raising up black Christian philosophers, thinkers, and others of truth who will address these ideologies at the root. These people of God will de-colonize and de-westernize our education—the education designed to keep us relegated to the bottom of the ladder.

In the process of developing our own educational system, we must de-Africanize some of our teaching. Animism and ancestral worship, which developed after we lost our biblical spiritual heritage through slavery, is still indirectly being taught. One of the characteristics of an oppressed people is that they end up worshiping the dead, because they have no hope in life or the living.

Furthermore, we have to deregulate education. We must take education out of the hands of the state. It is the state that dictates the way our children should think and even the way we should raise them. The only way we can win this war is with the Word of God.

We are members of the body of Christ. We are equipped to influence the world. We are salt and light. We are called to preserve this world and rid it of oppressive and barbaric systems. We cannot look to Western philosophy for our education, because it is full of information that opposes what God says about image, identity, destiny, and equality. We cannot turn to Western philosophies because in them man's thoughts are placed above God's thoughts. When man's thoughts are placed above God's thoughts, man makes up his own rules of how things should be run and thinks he's in control. Thus we have the evils of slavery and oppression as a part of the history of this nation.

My wife and I have made a commitment to God that none of our children will be educated at the feet of Satan's apostles. We are educating our own children. We are training them up in the admonition of the Lord. We are not only training our own children, but we are instrumental in educating other black children. The Lord blessed our church to start an academy, and we are seeing our children achieve at a level that the secular educators thought was not possible. Recently, two of our students won second place in a science fair. They are achieving because they are learning under a system that establishes a biblical foundation, reinforces God's purposes and destinies for their lives, and emphasizes a relationship with the Lord. We are prevailing in the fight solely because we are giving our children an education that is uncompromisingly biblical truth and unashamedly Christ-centered.

People have accepted that society must be made up of upper, middle, and lower classes. *Who said so? God didn't say that!*

WELFARE, A WAY OF LIFE

Another system that continues to affect black people is the welfare system, created in the 1930s because of the Depression. It was meant to be a temporary solution until people were able to get back on their feet. But it has become a way to entrap a people and keep them in a box. Uncle Sam has become the pimp of our black neighborhoods, handing out living expenses while dictating how people must live. He has corralled our women and treats them like whores, limiting their ability to achieve by paying them, month after month, year after year.

We are now into the fourth generation of welfare mothers in the black community. That monthly check paralyzes people's motivations to be productive. They remain consumers. Some want to do better, even try, but it's too difficult to get off welfare, to be on your own. It becomes a mentality.

I watched one lady who was on welfare all her life until her last child was eighteen. Welfare was cut off. She didn't know what to do. She had no idea how to live on her own. She was desperate, in constant fear, because there was no one to take care of her. She was a good lady, she just didn't know what to do. In a few years she died. She wasn't that old. She just didn't want to live anymore.

I've known grown children from these welfare homes unable to make it on their own. They stay with different people, living like a leech. They don't know the joys of working and having their own apartment, being in charge of their lives. What their mothers learned on welfare is carrying on to the next generation.

We have to break this dependency mentality. It stifles people and they end up getting locked into that system. Because of what it's created over the last sixty years, we can't just totally pull the rug out, but drastic reforms are needed. I almost blame the system that created it, because it gives the money without teaching them any skills, giving them any opportunity.

When the job market is poor, these welfare mothers know that a minimum wage job, by the time they pay babysitting and transportation expenses, brings in less than sitting at home waiting to collect a welfare check. There's a saying: Last to be hired, first to be fired. But to these unskilled workers, it's not just a saying. It's reality. And they stay on welfare out of fear, even though in their heart of hearts they don't want to do that.

One lady on welfare had scrimped and saved to be able to send her daughter to college. The money came from relatives, from gifts. She wanted to break the welfare cycle that had held her. About the time she had $3,000 in the bank, the welfare department found out about it and fined her $15,000! She was sentenced to a year or two in jail, though a judge suspended the sentence. The $3,000 went to pay part of her fine instead of her daughter's college tuition.

This mother had been frugal and saved, always keeping her focus on her daughter's future, on college. But she was too frugal. She legally could have only $1,500. The lesson you learn from this is to spend all your money so you can get more from the welfare department. That lesson is wrong. No wonder people can't get off welfare. The rules need to help you, not hurt you. This woman didn't do anything wrong. The rule was wrong.

The sad thing about this story is that this kind of control still exists. We cannot look to a system that has added to our problems to all of a sudden solve our problems. We must get out of that mentality. We have no choice but to depend on God.

The Gospel message has not touched these areas. We as a church coexist with some of society's ungodly practices. But we have to be free from the system to be able to effectively challenge the system. We have to be free or we cannot fulfill our role as a higher kingdom, a city set on a hill.

When the kingdom of God comes to a people, it will affect and overturn ungodly and evil systems. Therefore we must preach the pure Gospel of the kingdom of God. We must not be afraid to manifest the kingdom of God. The only way we can overturn these systems is through the preaching of the Gospel. We must challenge every system that has affected black people. Only then will the walls of classism and welfare come tumbling down.

Chapter 18

We Must Not Miss Our Season

One of the saddest phrases in Scripture to me is Luke 19:44b: "Thou knewest not the time of thy visitation."

Jesus' heart wept because the people of Israel did not recognize when God came to them through him. This phrase haunts me and has put a drive in me to reach the body of Christ, especially the black segment, with the truth of restoration of identity and the anointing of the Holy Spirit. We must not miss our season!

"To every thing there is a season, and a time to every purpose under heaven" (Ecclesiastes 3:1). This verse helps us to understand that all things, including movements, have seasons. I believe the black segment of the body of Christ, through the anointing of the Holy Spirit, is in a season of visitation, renewal, restoration, revival, and re-establishment of God's purpose for our lives.

We as a people have been forced to find a place in everyone else's purpose and we end up missing our own purpose. We have danced to everyone else's tune while our steps have become awkward to our own music. We have even forgotten what our tune sounds like.

I believe the Lord has given us a season to return to him and to stop trying to be something we are not. Jesus said, "I know whence I came, and whither I go" (John 8:14). The principle of his statement is very appropriate for today: If you don't know where you came from, it will be very difficult to know where you are going.

We are, through the anointing of the Holy Spirit, in a season of redefining and rediscovering who we are as a people through a proper interpretation of Biblical history. God has need of us to fulfill his purpose in the world, but he can't use us if we are trying to be something we are not. "The word of the LORD is right; and all his works are done in truth" (Psalm 33:4).

It is not impossible, but it is extremely difficult, for the Lord to work in our churches, neighborhoods, and our society if we are not moving and working in the power and ability of the Holy Spirit and being true to who and what we really are.

In this society, to boldly express our "blackness" is sometimes dangerous, and those who do may be labeled radicals. In many cases you are labeled as "normal" if you act like, and have the mannerisms and value system of, the white race. Blacks have learned more and more to conform to the dictates of life from a white perspective. We have become what is acceptable to the majority race in America and thus have been blinded to our *season of anointing*, thus forfeiting identity, purpose, and destiny.

This mentality is damaging to the purposes of God, especially when our ethnic group's appointed time comes.

We violate our candidacy for the anointing when we take on falsehood and identities other than our own, because the anointing comes by the agency of the Spirit of Truth. We have lived out lies and not been true to who we really are, and the Spirit of God is looking for truth and integrity.

There has never been a black Billy Graham, or a black Oral Roberts, or a black Kathryn Kuhlman or William Branhan. One reason that we have not produced ministers of this caliber is because many of us are praying for an anointing to be like one of these individuals, but God only anoints us to be like Christ and to be who we are in him, in our own ethnicity and culture. We have been taught so long to hate ourselves that we are not being true to who we are. Remember, "all his works are done in truth" (Psalm 33:4).

This is a season where the anointing of the Holy Spirit and the truth of the Word are being revealed, and the lies of Satan that have kept our people and society in bondage are being exposed and disposed of.

My brothers and sisters, let us arise, for we must not miss our season!